GIRLS SPEAK OUT

GIRLS SPEAK OUT

Finding Your True Self

Andrea Johnston

WITH AN INTRODUCTION
BY GLORIA STEINEM

SCHOLASTIC PRESS / NEW YORK

Excerpt on pp. 25-26 from the introduction to *Wonder Woman* by Gloria Steinem.
Copyright © 1995 by DC Comics. Reprinted by permission of DC Comics.
Excerpt on p. 28 from *Outrageous Acts and Everyday Rebellions* by Gloria Steinem.
Copyright © 1983 by the author. Reprinted by permission of the author.
Further acknowledgments, pp. 209-210.

Library of Congress Cataloging-in-Publication Data.
Johnston, Andrea.
Girls speak out: finding your true self / by Andrea Johnston; with an introduction by
Gloria Steinem.
p.   cm.
Includes bibliographical references (p. 209).
Summary: A handbook on self-esteem for girls.
ISBN 0-590-89795-0
1. Teenage girls—United States—Psychology—Juvenile literature.
2. Self-esteem in adolescence—United States—Juvenile literature.
3. Self-perception in adolescence—United States—Juvenile literature.
4. Self-esteem in women—United States—Juvenile literature.
5. Self-help groups—Activity programs—Juvenile literature.
[1. Self-esteem. 2. Self-perception. 3. Adolescence.] I. Title.
HQ798.J615   1996
155.5'33—dc20   96-14802

12 11 10 9 8 7 6 5   9/9 0 1 2/0

Printed in the U. S. A.   45
First edition, February 1997
Line illustrations by Dan Krovatin
Book design by Elizabeth B. Parisi

*To girls and their friends everywhere,
and to Gloria, Jesse, and Yulahlia,
for listening, believing, and trusting.*

Contents

Acknowledgments   xi

Introduction   xix

Openings   1

Naming Ourselves   5

Being Eleven   10

What's Different, What's the Same   17

Writing Ourselves into History   23

In Our Image   34

Finding a Place   60

Making Choices   68

Going into the Woods   83

The Green Stone   93

Together Again   105

Changing the System   120

Doing a Talk Show   136

Being a Daughter   146

Our True Selves   158

Closings and Beginnings   193

About the Ancient Artifacts   195

Further Reading   202

Further Acknowledgments   209

GIRLS SPEAK OUT

Acknowledgments

Acknowledgments in books usually thank people in words. A few days ago, as I was helping to celebrate Take Our Daughters To Work Day® at the Ms. Foundation for Women in New York City, an eight-year-old girl, Diamora, gave me one of the best thank yous I've ever received — and she did it without words.

I was talking with Diamora about that special place inside each of us where our unique, true self lives, where no one else can go, and where it's safe. We were face-to-face, focused on each other. Slowly, and deliberately, Diamora pointed her finger to her chest and as her finger moved, a smile grew. Her whole face lit up. I felt like I was showered in light.

Here is my acknowledgment in words, accompanied by Diamora's smile, to the children and grown-ups who made Girls Speak Out possible.

When Gloria Steinem and I decided to create a program for girls, we wanted to use prehistory to show other possibilities for female human beings. In order to make that idea come alive in girls' hands, I asked some friends to form a steering committee. We met in my house for about six months.

Four ex-students of mine became steering-committee teachers: Christina Dry, age 12, Elizabeth "Lizard" Foster-Shaner, age 11, Meghan Long, age 11, and Sarah Mascolo, age 12, talked, listened, laughed, read, sewed, ate, shopped, hiked, field-tested artifacts, and kept journals so that we could give other girls what they would like to experience. Nine-year-old Emily Luna and nineteen-year-old Pauline Greenfield also joined the group. Gail Dry, Teri Foster, Michelle Long, and Michelle Luna openly shared their experiences as well as their time with their daughters.

Pia Hamilton became a certified teacher, and Jan Moore left public school teaching as we developed "Girls Speak Out." Francine Kuney shared her concern for her grandchildren's future, and retired school librarian, Milly Lee, sold her first children's book as she looked for books for "Girls Speak Out."

In September 1994, we were ready to leave my house and go on the road. Our original name for the program was "Talks for Girls," a name that traveled with me until I returned home to finish this book. When we realized that "Talks for Girls" was too similar to other names already in circulation, my agent and lawyer, Bob Levine, asked his ten-year-old daughter, Joanna, a program participant, to brainstorm with us.

I'm grateful to Bob for his support and inspiration, and to Joanna for thinking of "Girls Speak Out."

After leaving my house I continued to meet women who work on behalf of girls. Joline Godfrey's advice about nationwide girls' programs was down-to-earth and inspiring. Jean Shinoda Bolen, MD, brainstormed about how we could be sure "Girls Speak Out" is a safe place for girls. Elizabeth Debold contributed her expertise after participating in one of our first sessions. Hallie Iglehart Austen searched for artifacts and brought the steering committee to her backyard labyrinth in Point Reyes, California.

Our first pilot program was held in our backyard, in Sonoma County, California. Then we traveled to the San Jose, California, YWCA, and principal Virginia Mcqueen brought students from her San Jose school. Kristina Kiehl and her daughter, Annie, were among our earliest and warmest supporters. Amelia Richards, chair of Third Wave, a nationwide organization of young feminists, organized "Girls Speak Out's" third and fourth pilot programs in the Third Wave's offices in New York City.

The Ms. Foundation for Women is one of the first collective voices for girls and women heard in this country, and with the help of its president, Marie Wilson, "Girls Speak Out" pilots became financially viable.

Tara Tremmel is one of "Girls Speak Out's" goddess-mothers: she has traveled with me to different states, videotaped hundreds of girls, and opened her heart to all of us.

"Girls Speak Out's" photographer is Jennifer Warburg, another goddess-mother to the program. Jennifer went from state to state, carrying more equipment than anyone should, in record-breaking heat and cold, to capture the range of feeling in the faces of the girls and women who've participated in the program.

Gail Maynor brought her joy — and Girl Scout troop — to the Ms. Foundation's offices for "Girls Speak Out" sessions.

In 1995, "Girls Speak Out" affiliated with the YWCA of the U.S.A. for a year to insure that sessions would be held in female-friendly places across the United States. Prema Mathai-Davis, Executive Director of the YWCA of the U.S.A., and Cindy Sutliff, Chief of Staff of the YWCA of the U.S.A., have given immeasurable support to "Girls Speak Out" — and a place for it to grow.

As I visited different YWCAs, I began to realize why Gloria and other feminists who work on a grassroots level are optimistic about what's happening in the women's movement. The women who organized sessions and worked with me at the following YWCA locations were an inspiration and a joy: I thank the staff and volunteers in Chicago, Illinois; Minneapolis,

Minnesota; San Diego, California; Portland, Oregon; Charleston, South Carolina; and Wheeling, West Virginia.

I'm grateful to Karen Genét and Valerie Romero of the San Diego YWCA, Tiffany Howard of the Charleston YWCA, and Susan Hogan of the Wheeling, West Virginia, YWCA, for their ongoing encouragement, ideas, and perspectives.

"Girls Speak Out" sessions have also been held in public housing in New York City. The I Have A Dream program in Chelsea-Elliot public housing became a "Girls Speak Out" site through the efforts of Kathleen Clarke-Glover, Director of the Office of Education, New York City Public Housing, and Roberta Stallings, Chief of Staff. Roberta advised me on this book, and her and Kathleen's continuing friendships are a welcome bonus.

Global Kids, Inc. is a community-based organization for girls and boys in high schools in New York City. Carole Nichols, Executive Director, and her staff responded eagerly to a feminist program for girls. I'm happy our two programs met and meshed so well.

"Girls Speak Out" inspired me to travel back to my own childhood, and I was fortunate to find people I felt and heard as a young girl who still speak from the heart. Marianne "Bunny" Cairo and Arlene Gold, my cousin and seventh- and eighth-grade teacher respectively, prove to me that if we look deep inside ourselves, we'll find love. I thank my mother for listening, even when she realized I was never good at keeping secrets. My nephews, Pedro, Daniel, and Peter, make me glad I live in the present.

Florence Howe, publisher of Feminist Press; Brenda Bowen, my editor; Heather Dietz, editorial assistant, and Alan Cohen, publicity director at Scholastic Inc., "got it" right away, and helped me understand I could write for and reach the solitary girl reader. I'm grateful to agent Felicia Eth because, among other things, she champions whistle-blowers: her attempts to educate the publishing world about sexual harassment in the schools, even as my book proposal on that topic received rejection after rejection, were instrumental in breaking down the walls of isolation I was experiencing in my local community.

Alice Walker's generosity and storytelling are touchstones in more ways than are visible in this book. I thank Anita Hill for reminding me of "magic" and how change takes patience, and Marcia Ann Gillespie for making sure I understood that being in the moment means listening to my own voice. Clarissa Pinkola Estés focused me inwards at a time when I was struggling to be all things to all people. Marlo Thomas' spirit, and her commitment to *Free to Be . . .* make me smile and keep on going. Nancy Rose and Karin Lippert knew more about how to make "Girls Speak Out" reach more girls, and they let me learn it, too.

Friends on both coasts came together to keep "Girls Speak Out," and me, moving: Hummingbird Berreyesa, John Boland, Jim Carroll, Chava Enos, Judy Glassman, Julius Kuney, Sharon Montoya, Jane and Charlie Sandbank, Cindy Tew, Sonja Tubridy, Bonnie and Bob Weinstein, and the "Girls Speak Out" steering committee gave me shelter, sometimes literally as well as figuratively. I hope they know how much I value their friendships.

Judy Weston allows me to hear myself, and to listen to others. Martha Baker is proof to me of past lives, because when we met recently, it was as sisters with a long, shared history.

My feminist son, Jesse, alternately advised me to "get over myself," and trust my instincts in developing "Girls Speak Out." Sometimes this meant risking where and how we lived for the sake of what he believes: that everyone matters.

My niece and goddess-daughter, Yulahlia, is a goddess-mother of "Girls Speak Out." She participated in sessions, and she inspires young girls who want to be their true selves, as she is. She expanded the focus of this book with her insights.

Gloria Steinem is a parent of "Girls Speak Out."

Maybe she knew what we were getting into — I have a suspicion she knew more than I did. I could not have a truer friend, collaborator, or editor.

She showed me that fundamental change takes stamina, and it comes from the heart. If this book has some of Gloria's spirit, we're blessed.

Thank you, parents and guardians, for sharing your daughters.

Thank you, girls, for being you.

Introduction

This book is for every girl who wants to find her true self, and for every friend of a girl who wants to help her. It's also a good book for grown-ups who work with girls, and for women who want to rediscover the girl who lives inside them.

Because a book is like a person, I'd like to tell you the story of how this book came to be:

I am a feminist organizer. That means I travel around the country, trying to help people who want to create more fairness for girls and women — which makes life better for boys and men, too. Sometimes the people are inside families or in schools, sometimes in the work-place or in our political system. I've been doing this for a very long time, longer than most of you reading this have been alive and maybe longer than your parents have been alive, so I've learned a lot.

I've learned that every person is important, and so is everything that happens to each person. In fact, a pretty good first step to almost any kind of change is looking at the world *as if everyone mattered.*

I've learned that we can do a lot more if we find people who believe in us, and talk to them as often as we can.

And I've learned that girls like you already have a unique strength and wisdom inside. I hope this book helps you to believe in your own wisdom, and listen to it.

One of the things I've also noticed is that people have an easier time imagining fairness in the future if they know that it existed in the past. Equality between girls and boys can't be "against nature," the way some very discouraged people say it is, because those ancient times and cultures that came before the history we usually study in school — which is why they are called "prehistory" — had much more balance between males and females. Thanks to feminist scholars and new scientific measurements that show many artifacts to be much older than experts originally thought (including some of the goddess figures you'll see in these pages), we know that, for about ninety-five percent of the time human beings have lived on earth, every continent had cultures in which girls were as valuable as boys, there were goddesses as well as gods, and men and women also lived in better balance with nature.

Of course, we can't go back to the past. But if everything we learn is about the last five percent of human history when males have been thought to be superior to females and one race has dominated another — which, I'm sorry to say, has been true for most people in the last few thousand years — then we're more likely to believe it's the natural or even the only way. As the saying goes, "If you've never seen a deer, it's hard to see a deer."

When I was growing up, for instance, I remember how hard it was for girls to stand up for ourselves, and to dream about a future that didn't depend on the men we might marry. Our families, our friends, our textbooks, and just about everything in our lives seemed to be saying: *Boys have always been more important — and they always will be.* Though we started out with a sense of fairness, as children do, the unfairness all around us made us feel alone, and sometimes a little crazy. (I bet there have been a lot of times when you, too, have said to yourself, "It isn't *fair!*") It was only after we were grown-ups that most of us began to talk to each other, discover we were neither alone nor crazy, and start a movement for a future in which women and girls could be strong, safe, and free.

For a long time, I'd been thinking about how much it would have meant to me — and how much it could mean to girls now — if this information about ancient times were part of everyday life. The problem was that

only people who were old enough to go to college
learned it — providing they took women's studies or
some other remedial course — or people like me, who
had time to read books after college.

Then one day, I learned something from my friend
Wilma Mankiller, the first woman to be elected Principal Chief of the Cherokee Nation. The ancient Cherokee tradition of balance between women and men, girls
and boys, had been reawakened by her election. I knew
that, just as a Council of Grandmothers used to choose
the male chief and decide when to go to war and when
to make peace, Wilma's leadership symbolized a return
to this balance that had been lost when the U.S. Government drove the Cherokees off their land, made fun
of their "petticoat government," and kept them from
teaching their language in their own schools — even
into the 1960s. What I didn't know was that Wilma had
also made a portable timeline and flash cards of Cherokee history, so it could be taken to small groups, even if
they lived deep in the countryside. She said that they
were helped by knowing about their past power and
culture, and understanding how they had been lost —
especially because they had been made to feel at fault
for their own poverty and lack of power. They gained
pride in themselves, and a belief that they could help
themselves.

Listening to Wilma convinced me that even a glimpse

of ancient female power could help girls of all races and cultures to believe in themselves, too. Just as Wilma had taken this information around to small groups, I imagined taking it to the kind of small groups that had given birth to the women's movement; groups called consciousness-raising, rap, or support groups, where women learned from each other's experiences.

Of course, I realized that girls as young as nine or ten probably couldn't go to meetings on their own, so there would have to be women there, too. But I also knew how important those ages were. Girls are clear-eyed and more truly themselves without the "feminine" role that arrives at twelve or so and creates a need to pretend. It had been my experience that girls of nine or ten not only reminded teenage girls of their true selves, but they reminded grown-up women, too. Besides, if those grown-ups were willing to answer girls' questions honestly, that would be important, too. I remembered how much I had longed to have my questions taken seriously, and how often I still met young girls who lack the chance to learn from a variety of grown-up women.

As I traveled around the country, I began to talk about this dream for girls and women. I talked about my hope that the inspiring knowledge of ancient history could get out of books and campuses, and into everyday life. This is what organizers do: we carry ideas and encouragement from one group to another, so everybody doesn't have to reinvent the wheel for themselves. Still, no dream becomes a reality until it finds someone who wants to act on it — which is as it should be.

About three years ago when I had just about decided this particular dream wasn't meant to come true, I was speaking in a big bookstore in a small town in northern California. Andrea Johnston, the woman you are about to meet in these pages, came up afterward, and talked more about starting such groups.

As a lifelong writer and activist on girls' and women's issues who was teaching the sixth, seventh, and eighth grades, she was one of the rare grown-ups who talked honestly with girls and was trusted by them. She had even helped several girls to speak out about a male teacher who was sexually harassing them; that is, touching and talking to them in a sexual way that made them feel uncomfortable. Andrea had become one of the first teachers in the country to support students in a case like this.

She and I met several more times to brainstorm about the kind of group that would have helped us when we were growing up, and to share what we had learned from girls about what would help them now. I realized that she could make this dream come true.

After carrying seeds around for a long time, I had found a gardener.

Over the next months, Andrea invited diverse groups of girls and women into her home, and tried out talks, games, artifacts, and many ways of sharing each other's wisdom. We brainstormed after each meeting. Eventually, these groups began to blossom on their own, and the wind of interest spread the seeds of this dream far and wide. Groups were held in thirteen cities and towns across the country, usually during one whole day on two consecutive weekends. Each time, Andrea traveled to be the gardener. When she returned, we would brainstorm some more, and think of ways to plant more gardens. Thanks to the Ms. Foundation for Women, a place where girls are a priority — for instance, the Ms. Foundation invented Take Our Daughters To Work Day,® the only national day devoted to girls — there was a foundation that could accept contributions for this project. Thanks to the YWCA of the U.S.A., there were safe places for girls and women to meet nationwide. Soon, there was a garden growing on its own.

I know you're wondering just what the groups are like, so you can make them your own through the pages of this book. They are a combination of what I imagined, what Andrea created from her long experience with girls, and what girls themselves have invented — and they also have a life of their own. You will experience them here in a very personal and detailed way, so I will just tell you some general things. For instance:

AGES: The groups, like this book, are for girls from nine to fifteen, though that is just a guideline. As Carol Gilligan has demonstrated with her research as a psychologist at Harvard University, girls at the younger end of that spectrum have their true voice, older ones have experienced the role that is coming, and both tend to learn from each other. Together, they "strengthen healthy rebellion," in Gilligan's phrase, and deal with such problems as the loss of freedom at twelve or so, just as boys are beginning to gain freedom.

The presence of women not only may offer a girl her first chance to ask an older woman questions, but she may also learn that questioning is part of every stage of life, and that grown-up women don't have all the answers either. For women, listening to girls' true voices often reawakens the rebellious girl within, helps them to realize the price paid when that little girl was "shushed," and see that she needn't be silenced anymore. Women also become more aware of the danger of silencing girls in the present.

Andrea also discovered that young women in their

late teens or early twenties could play a special role. They represent the next stage of life for nine-to-fifteen-year-olds, yet are close enough in age and experience to have great credibility. Two or three young women often serve as facilitators.

DIVERSITY: Just as a variety of ages offer more chances for each girl to expand her world, so do different races, classes, lifestyles, and abilities. That had been my experience as an organizer, and Andrea's as a teacher, so from the beginning, each group has included different races, economic groups, and backgrounds; from girls who live in housing projects to girls who board at private schools, from girls who speak two languages to girls whose real language is drawing or music. Near the beginning of the first day, Andrea sometimes asks a question: "What is different about us — and what is the same?" Or: "Go up to the girl who seems most different from you, and ask the question you're most afraid to ask." Usually, girls discover how many identities each girl has, and how hard it is to tell what's inside from what's outside.

Talking about goddesses and ancient history from every culture and part of the world also leads to understanding diversity. At a session where I was in New York, for instance, Andrea shaped seven big pieces of colored cloth like the seven continents, put them on the floor, and asked each girl to stand on the one she identified with — either because her family came from there, or because she just felt drawn to it. In that setting, we all knew that, if there was a continent without a girl on it, the world was not complete.

USING ALL FIVE SENSES: Since I am an inside-my-head kind of person, I had to learn from Andrea the importance of starting out with physical games that everyone can do; for instance, a simple game of clapping in different rhythms. When diverse girls do one thing together, they feel more like a group. If each of us uses our whole body, we also feel more whole. While you're reading this book, for example, you might do something physical every once in a while, like dancing or some exercise. There is no separation between our minds and our bodies. We all learn better when all five senses are alert.

Instead of just reading about ancient goddesses from all different cultures, for instance, we found replicas that girls can touch, pass around, make up stories about, and see how images of female power make them feel — just as girls in ancient times did. The girls also do lots of hands-on, all-five-senses things, like using clay, paints, and markers, keeping journals — just about every form of expression.

My favorite is using our voices to read aloud and tell

stories. After all, stories have been used to teach for thousands of years, because they take us on a journey instead of presenting us with a conclusion; they let us imagine ourselves in someone else's shoes; and they make clear that no situation is quite like any other. At the end of the first day, for instance, we always read *Finding the Green Stone* by Alice Walker, a story that inspired us to find many more. We also give each girl a green stone to symbolize her true self.

After all, we have to be truthful about how hard life is sometimes. But we also need to know there is a special place inside each of us where no one else can go. A place we can hold onto, like the green stone.

If Andrea and I have learned anything over these past few years, it's how unique each girl is, yet how much she affects and is affected by everyone around her. I think that's the secret we want to share with you: we are independent and interdependent. Each of us is unique, but we need a community that supports that uniqueness.

I hope these groups will be the beginning of a national, grassroots movement that belongs to girls; a whole country blooming with young voices and faces that have never been heard or seen before. There will also be spirits of the past helping these groups, from

Cherokee girls who roamed the plains in freedom, to your mothers and grandmothers who met in consciousness-raising groups to recover their freedom.

This book you hold in your hands is a new way of spreading seeds. But what happens must be what *you* want to happen. Now, you are the gardener *and* the flower.

Openings

I'm sitting by myself writing to you and you are probably sitting by yourself reading, yet we're not alone. We're connected by the words in this book. Words are a way of touching each other when we are not in the same room — or in the same time.

When I was growing up, I used to run away in books. Sometimes I was escaping from something bad that was happening. I wanted to enter a world where I could fly over the city, and plan how to be whoever I wanted to be.

I knew I could do whatever I wanted to do, even if I was a girl. People told me girls were supposed to just watch, and help out, because we couldn't do a lot of the best stuff. They are wrong about us. We can do whatever we want to do. We just need to learn how powerful we are and be reminded of how powerful women once were.

When I was ten years old, I did run away from home because I thought I wouldn't be allowed to be who I was. I had a new baby brother whom everyone thought was special simply because he was a boy, and after having two daughters my parents "finally had a son." The adults around me were being *sexist,* that is, they were judging us by our sex and deciding boys were better than girls. I love my brother, but I didn't like the feeling that I was a disappointment because I was born a girl, so I left a note for my parents hidden inside one of my favorite books, an illustrated copy of *Alice in Wonderland.* They never found the note, of course, and I came back before they missed me, hungry for lunch. Today, books are still the place to find messages. They're like coming home for me.

Now I'm grown-up. Even my son, Jesse, is grown-up. But I'm living my life with books as a writer and teacher. So you see, sometimes the things we love when we are very young can help to tell us who we are. Our true self never changes. Like a seed that grows into one particular flower: the wisdom is always inside.

But in the last two years, I've found a new way to connect girls, books, and women, just as I wished I could myself be connected when I was growing up. A friend, Gloria, and I created a special program for young girls. As we developed this program, we learned that we can walk into a room of girls and women we don't know, and before the day is over, we've become friends who trust and help each other.

Gloria and I are feminists. That means we believe

everyone matters; for instance, that girls are as important as boys, that no one race is more important than another, and that all people can make decisions for themselves. Feminism is a word that includes everyone: I think of it as an "and" word, meaning "girls *and* boys," instead of "girls *or* boys," or "black *and* white women" instead of "black *or* white women."

The problem is that girls aren't treated as equals to boys. To some degree, in all countries in the world, males are treated better than females because of an old and wrong belief that males are superior. That's why girls need to know they're strong, that the unfair system we live in is the problem. In other words, girls are okay, but a lot of the system isn't. Girls of color usually know this at an earlier age than white girls, because judging people by their skin color has been as much a problem as judging people by whether they're male or female — and now, it is at least recognized as wrong.

The special program we created is for girls nine to fifteen years old because that's the important change-over time from being a child to being a grown-up. It's called "Girls Speak Out." Older girls and women participate, too, by sharing their experiences of growing up so that young girls can see many different kinds of experiences, and have their questions answered. We talk about a time long ago, before the history you probably learn in school, when female people were as powerful

"We believe everyone matters."
— Andrea

and honored as male people, and even the gods were often women.

We do this because we want girls to know the way things are now is not the way things always were, or the way they always have to be in the future. No matter what, we are going to create a world in which each individual girl is powerful. In this world, boys would also be free to be who *they* really are. But it helps a lot to know that things were not always the way they are now, and there was once a time when females were honored — and so were nature and all living things.

"Girls Speak Out" is an experience we have in a room with other girls and women. Even if you can't be in this room with us, you can have some of the same experiences with this book. I hope its pages are a place to find and hold onto your true self. You can hear your own voice talking to others in these pages. This book can also connect you with the voices of other girls who believe in their true selves, and with women who feel the same way even after they've grown up.

You can use this book to organize a "Girls Speak Out" program after you've read about what we do. Or maybe reading about "Girls Speak Out" is enough. In either case, this book is a place you can visit whenever you want, like a memory. You can choose how to use it now and as you're growing up. It belongs to you.

I f you and I were in the same room now, the kind of room I do "Girls Speak Out" in, I think you'd be surprised by the lack of chairs or tables. "Girls Speak Out" breaks rules — like having to sit at desks or in chairs — which sometimes make us feel uncomfortable and keep us separated. We don't usually do "Girls Speak Out" in schools or places where people go to worship because these places need different rules than we do. We sit or stretch out on the floor most of the time we're together.

"Girls Speak Out" happens on two consecutive Saturdays, and it lasts for five hours each day, usually from 10 A.M. to 3 P.M. It's free. We play games, talk, eat, draw, write, work with clay, do a talk show, and talk some more about experiences we're having as we grow up.

When you look around the "Girls Speak Out" room, you see twelve or thirteen other girls from the ages of nine to fifteen. There are usually five or six older girls and women, some who come with the girls and some who are just interested in the program. A few of them, like the girls around your age, may look familiar from school or where you live, and others may be new to you. When it's possible, the group has girls and women of different races, cultures, classes, abilities, and sexual orientation, because the more different experiences there are, the more everybody has to learn from.

You're wearing a name tag you've written your name on with a colored marker. Some of the girls probably have the name tags on their shirts, some of them will put them on their pants, and one girl in Minneapolis, Minnesota, stuck hers on upside down so she could read it and look at the stars she decorated her name with.

The name tags are important because we use them in a game we play before we sit down and talk. The game we play with name tags introduces us to each other. My name tag says "Andrea" in green because it's a special color for me. What color would you choose for your name? Would you use more than one color? One color for each letter?

Now is a good time to get some pieces of paper or a small notebook you can write or draw in. That way, you'll be going through the same steps as you would if we were in the same room. If you're ready, you can write your name as you want it to look. Draw a shape and put your name inside it. It can be straight or curved or look like a puddle. After all, it's your name tag.

If you have a friend who's reading *Girls Speak Out,* you can write or draw messages to each other on certain pages in your notebooks. If you like being a solitary reader, talk to your notebook as if it's a diary or a journal. If you decide you want to show it to someone, you can always share it with a friend. And since I love being a reader, you can send your writings and/or drawings to me. There are many ways to share with yourself and with other girls and women. You make the choices.

You can imagine playing the name tag game with your friends and you can be the leader. A twenty-three-year-old woman named Anastasia taught us the game. She asked all the girls and women to stand in a circle. There are usually as many females in the circle as we have fingers and toes, about twenty of us all together, counting you and me. If it's any more than that, there isn't enough time for each person to be heard and for everybody to learn from each other. First, we have to make sure we can see each person's name tag.

We go around the circle and say our names out loud so we can hear how to say them. Some girls have unusual names like "Wislene" or "Casha." You'll see a lot of girls' names throughout these pages. You may want to say them out loud.

If two people have the same name we figure out what to call each person. In West Virginia, where a girl

"This woman's name is Kauo. Kauo is an old woman. She's about 20,000 years old."
—Shanuka

and a woman both had the name Kathryn, the girl liked to be called "Kat" and the woman stayed with Kathryn. Once we hear and practice saying each other's names, we're ready to move forward. It's important to call each person what she likes to be called so we practice doing these things right away.

Someone, usually me, who knows the game, or you — because you're reading this and now you'll know it, too — claps her hands and says someone else's name out loud. When we clap, we point our hands at the girl whose name we're saying. Then it's her turn to clap at another girl and say her name. The game continues like this until we build up speed, and it sounds like we're all clapping together. Or sometimes some girls and women will try different clapping rhythms.

In New York City, fifteen-year-old Rennie decided to stand in the center of the circle and close her eyes. Then she clapped each person's name from memory as she turned around in the circle. I think changing the rules is fun because it makes the game belong to you. The "Girls Speak Out" name tag game is invented again and again so it's always original, like each one of you.

Once we decide we know each other's names — and we're clapped out — we take some juice and fruit or muffins and come to sit on the floor in a circle. It's okay to eat and drink during the sessions — it makes us feel more comfortable if we know we can eat when we're hungry. I hope you can eat while you read if you like. I snack when I read. Even when I was teaching in public school, students in my room could eat snacks during reading time.

Being Eleven

I begin the "Girls Speak Out" circle by reading out loud. Stories are a signal for everyone to share an experience together.

When you see words written like this it means you'll be reading a story. In our sessions, everyone comes together to listen. One of the special things about reading this book is that I've included more stories than I can tell in one session. I usually choose stories depending on who's in the room. You can choose your favorites from the broad selection in this book, and you can also make up your own stories to write in your notebook.

We listen to the storyteller as we sit together on the floor. It's as if the storyteller is linking us with her voice. After the first storytelling, girls can take turns being storytellers. You, too, can read aloud from the story excerpts throughout the book.

The first story I read is a short story by one of my favorite writers named Sandra Cisneros. She's Mexican-American and she grew up in Chicago, a city with many separate neighborhoods where people of different colors and cultures live.

Sometimes when people look at other people, they just see their bodies, not who they really are inside. And sometimes they decide they want to stay away from anyone who looks a certain way because they've been told those people are different or bad. That's a problem with the person who's looking, not the one being looked at.

One of these problems is called *racism*. It means judging people by their race or skin color. Actually, skin color is determined by how much of a chemical called melanin we have in our skin. The more melanin, the darker the skin.

Another problem is called *classism*. That happens when people make decisions about other people based on how much money they have, or how poor they are, or by their family's status. *Sexism* is when people are judged by whether they're male or female. *Ageism* can be a problem, too. You can see how silly this is by inventing something. For instance, *chinism,* if there was such a thing, would be a way of judging someone by how much bone and flesh there is on her or his jaw.

We learn a lot about age and also about what happens when older people think they always know better than younger ones, in this story, "Eleven," from Cisneros' book, *Woman Hollering Creek.*

What they don't understand about birthdays and what they never tell you is that when you're eleven, you're also ten, and nine, and eight, and seven, and six, and five, and four, and three, and two, and one. And when you wake up on your eleventh birthday you expect to feel eleven, but you don't. You open your eyes and everything's just like yesterday, only it's today. And you don't feel eleven at all. You feel like you're still ten. And you are — underneath the year that makes you eleven.

Like some days you might say something stupid, and that's the part of you that's still ten. Or maybe some days you might need to sit on your mama's lap because you're scared, and that's the part of you that's five. And maybe one day when you're all grown up maybe you will need to cry like if you're three, and that's okay. That's what I tell Mama when she's sad and needs to cry. Maybe she's feeling three.

Because the way you grow old is kind of like an onion or like the rings inside a tree trunk or like my little wooden dolls that fit one inside the other, each year inside the next one. That's how being eleven years old is.

You don't feel eleven. Not right away. It takes a few days, weeks even, sometimes months before you say Eleven when they ask you. And you don't feel smart eleven, not until you're almost twelve. That's the way it is.

Only today I wish I didn't have only eleven years rattling inside me like pennies in a tin Band-Aid box. Today I wish I was one hundred and two instead of eleven because if I was one hundred and two I'd have known what to say when Mrs. Price put the red sweater on my desk. I would've known how to tell her it wasn't mine instead of just sitting there with that look on my face and nothing coming out of my mouth.

"Whose is this?" Mrs. Price says, and she holds the red sweater up in the air for all the class to see. "Whose? It's been sitting in the coatroom for a month."

"Not mine," says everybody. "Not me."

"It has to belong to somebody," Mrs. Price keeps saying, but nobody can remember. It's an ugly sweater with red plastic buttons and a collar and sleeves all stretched out like you could use it for a jump rope. It's maybe a thousand years old and even if it belonged to me I wouldn't say so.

Maybe because I'm skinny, maybe because she doesn't like me, that stupid Sylvia Saldivar says, "I think it belongs to Rachel." An ugly sweater like that, all raggedy and old, but Mrs. Price believes her. Mrs. Price takes the sweater and puts it right on my desk, but when I open my mouth nothing comes out.

"That's not, I don't, you're not...Not mine," I finally say in a little voice that was maybe me when I was four.

"Of course it's yours," Mrs. Price says. "I remember you wearing it once." Because she's older and the teacher, she's right and I'm not.

Not mine, not mine, not mine, but Mrs. Price is already turning to page thirty-two, and math problem number four. I don't know why but all of a sudden I'm feeling sick inside, like the part of me that's three wants to come out of my eyes, only I squeeze them shut tight and bite down on my teeth real hard and try to remember today I am eleven, eleven. Mama is making a cake for me tonight, and when Papa comes home everybody will sing Happy birthday, happy birthday to you.

But when the sick feeling goes away and I open my eyes, the red sweater's still sitting there like a big red mountain. I move the red sweater to the corner of my desk with my ruler. I move my pencil and books and eraser as far from it as possible. I even move my chair a little to the right. Not mine, not mine, not mine.

In my head I'm thinking how long till lunchtime, how long till I can take the red sweater and throw it over the schoolyard fence, or leave it hanging on a parking meter, or bunch it up into a little ball and toss it in the alley. Except when math period ends Mrs. Price says loud and in front of everybody, "Now, Rachel, that's enough," because she sees I've shoved the red sweater to the tippy-tip corner of my desk and it's hanging all over the edge like a waterfall, but I don't care.

"Rachel," Mrs. Price says. She says it like she's getting mad. "You put that sweater on right now and no more nonsense."

"But it's not —"

"Now!" Mrs. Price says.

This is when I wish I wasn't eleven, because all the years inside of me — ten, nine, eight, seven, six, five, four, three, two, and one — are pushing at the back of my eyes when I put one arm through one sleeve of the sweater that smells like cottage cheese, and then the other arm through the other and stand there with my arms apart like if the sweater hurts me and it does, all itchy and full of germs that aren't even mine.

That's when everything I've been holding in since this morning, since when Mrs. Price put the sweater on my desk, finally lets go, and all of a sudden I'm crying in front of everybody. I wish I was invisible but I'm not. I'm eleven and it's my birthday today and I'm crying like I'm three in front of everybody. I put my head down on the desk and bury my face in my stupid clown-sweater arms. My face all hot and spit coming out of my mouth because I can't stop the little animal noises from coming out of me, until there aren't any more tears left in my eyes, and it's just my body shaking like when you have the hiccups, and my whole head hurts like when you drink milk too fast.

But the worse part is right before the bell rings for lunch. That stupid Phyllis Lopez, who is even dumber than Sylvia Saldivar, says she remembers the red sweater is hers! I take it off right away and give it to her, only Mrs. Price pretends like everthing's okay.

Today I'm eleven. There's a cake Mama's making for tonight, and when Papa comes home from work we'll eat it. There'll be candles and presents and everyone will sing Happy birthday, happy birthday to you, Rachel, only it's too late.

I'm eleven today. I'm eleven, ten, nine, eight, seven, six, five, four, three, two, and one, but I wish I was one hundred and two. I wish I was anything but eleven, because I want today to be far away already, far away like a runaway balloon, like a tiny *o* in the sky, so tiny-tiny you have to close your eyes to see it.

Birthdays can be exciting and confusing. The idea that each birthday means adding another year to who we are means we are building on our past experiences. If the youngest person reading this book or doing a "Girls Speak Out" session is nine years old and the oldest is fifty-one, like me, then we all share what can happen from one through nine years old. No matter how old we are or how different, each of us has her beginning years to share, think, talk, and write about.

Now we are ready to share more about ourselves by going around the circle and telling our names, ages, and something we want the group to know about us, something the other girls and women probably couldn't guess by looking.

As the girls and women tell their ages, it surprises some girls: one time, one of the girls said "Whoa" each time and she made us laugh after a few "Whoas." Sometimes what we think an age looks like isn't what someone really looks like. And girls and women don't always tell their ages, because many people in this culture behave as if girls aren't valuable when they're really little, and women are worth less as they get older. That's what *ageism* is. It's taboo to tell your age, as if being old is embarrassing.

I've learned from girls that knowing how long someone has lived means we can look forward to getting older and collecting experiences that we can share about life. Janine, who's thirteen, asked why her age surprised everyone and it was because she's so tall. She

"I am going to be forty-seven years old and I am being reborn."

—Rebecca

thought she had to act older and it was funny to think she was expected to "act her height" as well as her age.

When I say I'm fifty-one, girls are usually very surprised because that seems so old to them. *I'm* surprised that I've been alive so many years, too. I used to think life stopped when you got old and now I'm learning it keeps getting new. And when I say that I think being nine or ten means knowing what's fair and thinking you can be anything you want to be, most girls agree, especially girls who are at or close to those ages.

It's challenging to figure out what you want someone to know about you that they couldn't guess. What is important to you that you want other people to know but isn't easy to see? Making lists of what words describe you and what you like to do could show what is unique about you, because each of us is a unique mixture of many things.

Soon, we get to things that are even less visible than age. An eleven year old told us she was adopted. Another girl said her parents were divorced and she wants to use her mother's and her father's last names to show she comes from both of them. Another girl told us her sister was handicapped and she's learned from her sister that handicapped people are like anyone else.

Girls do a lot of things: one girl said she rode horses, another said she studied karate, some girls read a lot, and some girls played sports, especially basketball. Two sisters talked about growing up in Trinidad, where they were born. A sixteen year old said she lived in an apartment in public housing in Chicago and she didn't feel safe going outside alone except to go to school. One girl said she had a boyfriend and another girl said she wanted one. Some girls said they aren't really interested in boys yet. One fifteen-year-old girl said she liked being with girls better than boys.

A woman in South Carolina said she wanted to make better connections with her thirteen-year-old daughter. Another woman in South Carolina, a teacher and a minister named Helen, told us about being the first black student to go to a state college. She grew up in an all-black town because white people had segregated it — that is, they wouldn't let black people live where white people did — but she hadn't realized why. Being with white people when she went away to college was new to her. She was shocked to realize they didn't like her: she was hit by water from high-pressure hoses by whites who didn't want her in the same college with them. The first night she was away at school, the police told her she had to sleep in the jail in order to be safe. She still remembers that the police didn't let her call her family and her parents worried all night because they didn't know where she was. That still makes her angry today.

Natalie, a ten-year-old girl, told Helen she had read

a story about a boy who was a slave during the Civil War. Natalie said she couldn't understand why people are cruel to other people just because of their color. "It doesn't make sense to me. It's not logical that people care so much about skin color," she said. Skin color is something girls talk about when we look at our group of girls and women and that's why it's good to be diverse — you learn more about things.

In Chicago, everyone in the room except me was African-American, and when I asked the girls to talk about what was the same about us, Tiffany, who is twelve years old, surprised me by saying, "We're all black." For a moment, it was quiet in the room. Then one of the women said, "No, Andrea's white." Tiffany just shrugged her shoulders and said, "Oh, I thought she was light-skinned."

When I asked what was different about us as a group, one girl listed all the different colors of our clothes and different types of shoes. When you think about what's different about you and girls you know best, like sisters or friends, what kinds of things come to your mind? Is it mostly things we can see like body size, hairstyles, and clothes? Do you imagine we're different on the inside? You can keep these thoughts in mind as you read what other girls and women say and write about their feelings and think about what you want to say and write about yours.

As a young girl, I didn't learn what's memorable about women from textbooks or classroom discussions because female human beings were rarely mentioned in what I studied. But I did have some great women teachers who cared about me and understood me more than anyone else did. My seventh-grade and eighth-grade teacher and my high school teacher showed me that there could be something special and exciting about being a woman, including reaching out to girls. One of those teachers, my middle school teacher, Arlene, even helped with this book by suggesting stories for girls to read.

Are there any girls or women who inspire you? Girls often say they want to talk to and trust women. One young woman said her father had "raised" her not to trust women because her mother had left him when she was three. She was glad to meet women in "Girls Speak Out" who made her feel good about herself and them. We find women different ways: sometimes they're our mothers or in our family, sometimes they're teachers, and sometimes girls find women in books who help us believe we're okay and not alone.

How many women or girls can you remember learning about from history books or classroom discussions? When I ask this question in "Girls Speak Out" sessions, we usually discover that there are too few females written about in history, especially females of color. Even the pictures on walls in auditoriums, school hallways, and classrooms are generally of white men like the ones called the Founding Fathers of this country. In fact, girls and women are over half the human population, and we're part of everything that happens. As one girl said, "I want girls to finally be treated as equals. We need to learn how to get the power around to girls and women."

Females are missing from history books and discussions, but it's not because we didn't do anything important. We're missing from history because people who write the textbooks, and many teachers and people who make decisions about what's important in history leave us out. That's why there's no mention of the fact that there were places and times when females shared or took control. And no mention of women's contributions to their communities. That's one of the reasons why I put the girls' and women's writings from each session into a book. Everyone gets a copy. It's a new kind of girls' and women's history book.

Nine-year-old Karen in New York says that "all those history books in school and libraries are written without us." Twelve-year-old Sarah in California agrees: "Boys already have history written down for them and it's in their favor." But when we write down our experiences, we see that they're history, too.

Writing Ourselves into History

Remember: history is happening right this very second, but it disappears with each second unless we decide to remember it and to say what happened. Then we can give it a name, just like we name ourselves. Historians use words like "revolution" or "movement" when a lot of people decide to solve a problem they're tired of living with. In addition, we can write history about the feelings of a Mexican-American girl turning eleven at the end of the twentieth century. That's what Sandra Cisneros did.

Our story as a human race began thousands of years ago, a long time before books existed. How does a girl learn without books? The same way Tiffany in Chicago does when she looks around a room; she looks, thinks, and says what's on her mind. She's making her own observations. She's a historian. We can look at remnants of ancient times, too.

Prehistory is the name given to the experiences of people who lived before what we know as writing was invented. Prehistory got along before the *patriarchy*. A patriarchy is a system in which men dominate women and children. All of us — children, women, men, and nature — are living in a patriarchy now. It's been the system for the last five thousand years or so, depending on which part of the world you live in — but that's much less than five percent of the time that people have been on earth.

Today, we're only taught written history so we think it's what's "natural" and "normal" for us to feel and believe. But ninety-five percent of human history happened in prehistory, before there were books, and we're learning more and more from ruins and bones, cave paintings, and oral legends — many things.

There are a lot of supposed-tos that girls talk about in "Girls Speak Out." A supposed-to can be a rule that's written down. It can be an unwritten rule. It's something we're told we should want to do, but it doesn't always feel right. For instance, girls feel they should pretend they're not as smart as the boys in their classes so the boys will like them or not make fun of them.

It's easy to become confused, as I was as a child, and think there is something wrong with you because everyone else seems to go along with the system. I liked knowing the answers in school, especially when I had tried hard to figure things out, but I remember sitting there knowing boys would be called on first — and more often — than any of the girls. And that it was more okay for them to argue or say what they thought.

Patriarchal history — which is another word for most written history — confuses many girls and women and makes us invisible.

But *prehistory is filled with other possibilities.*

There are surprises in imagining possibilities. Have you ever heard of Wonder Woman? You might think of her as a modern comic book heroine, dressed in red, white, and blue, but she's also an example of how we can go into the past and create ideas for a new present and future. Because, as you'll see, even this comic book figure had a beginning in prehistory.

Wonder Woman has a mission, to change "a world torn by the hatreds and wars of men." She does it without killing her enemies. Wonder Woman believes in peace, equality, self-reliance, and respect for others. What's "historical" about her is that she's modeled on an Amazon, a member of what may have been a race of superhuman women from thousands of years ago.

As my friend Gloria wrote in an introduction to a book about the origins of Wonder Woman, " . . . there's . . . evidence . . . Amazon societies were real; they did exist. . . . In the jungles of Brazil, German and Brazilian scientists found caves of what appears to have been an all-female society. . . . Such myths and archaeological finds have turned up not only along the

"Hi, I'm Cleopatra's baby."
—Lydia

Amazon River in Brazil, but at the foot of the Atlas Mountains in northwestern Africa, and on the European and Asiatic sides of the Black Sea. . . .

"Rather than give up freedom [when patriarchy began to rule women] and worship only male gods, some bands of women resisted. They formed all-women cultures. . . . In Europe, graves once thought to contain male skeletons — because they were buried with weapons, or killed by battle wounds — have turned out to contain skeletons of females after all."

One of the earliest skeletons found by scientists is an African woman named "Lucy" by those who found her, and she's thousands of years old. She did a lot of the same wonderful things we do today: she walked on the same earth under the same sky. Our skin colors evolved from Lucy's color, which was black, to all the different shades we see around us today.

If we travel back in time to Lucy's eleventh birthday, which is as far back as we have any remains of human history, there were many girls and women. Without us, there is no history or human race. Just as we do, Lucy saw females around her get older, go from place to place, and change in size and shape. She watched sunsets and sunrises, she could see the moon appear to swallow the sun during a total eclipse, and she saw crescent moons, half moons, and full moons.

At night, sleeping outside, moonlight would shine

on Lucy's face like a night-light. As the moon changed shape, from a sliver to a full moon, it would shine different amounts of light on her face. These cycles of the moon, as it goes from crescent to full, are about a month long. And a girl like Lucy thousands of years ago would have noticed something about the girls and women around her.

Once a month, some girls and women would bleed — but they weren't hurt and they didn't die. Month after month, they had these periods, and they would bleed and be okay. Menstruation was magic. It happened with a rhythmic cycle similar to the cycle of the moon. I think it seemed to Lucy as if there's a connection between us on the ground and something far away in the sky. It isn't a connection we can see or touch, but it's something we can imagine has special meaning, and gives us a special connection to a big and important thing, like the way the earth turns in its solar system.

Perhaps Lucy welcomed having her period because it made her feel powerful enough to connect with the moon in the sky.

Today girls have different experiences with their periods. In one "Girls Speak Out" session a girl in San Diego, California, asked if it makes any difference how old a girl is before she starts her period. Each female in the room had started menstruating at a different age.

One girl talked about designing a cramps doll to hold in your hand and squeeze when you have cramps. Girls talk about hiding tampons and sanitary napkins in their backpacks and pockets because it would be embarrassing if boys found them. They said they were ashamed of having their period and kept their time of the month a secret. When one group is supposed to be superior, then whatever happens to the other group is inferior.

That's the way things are now for females. What would it be like if they changed? Let's imagine that women didn't get their periods, but men did. Gloria wondered what would happen "If Men Could Menstruate?" in an article she wrote almost twenty years ago. If men are considered superior, would getting a period just be something else that's considered superior, too? If they got their periods, Gloria decided, "Men would brag about how long and how much.

"Young boys would talk about it as the envied beginning of manhood. Gifts, religious ceremonies, family dinners and . . . parties would mark the day. . . ." Doing reversals, like Alice in Wonderland's walking in the wrong direction to get to the right place, is one of the ways we can change how we understand things. All you have to do is imagine that something being said to you was being said to a boy, or something said about white people was said about people of color.

Can you imagine celebrating your period? We don't have to imagine ourselves back in Lucy's time to find people who celebrate menstruation. Native American girls and women come from very old cultures and they have ceremonies to mark a girl's period and welcome this new part of her life. Gina, a mother of two girls in northern California, worked with me in designing "Girls Speak Out." She thought the idea of celebrating your period was a good one, so when her older daughter, Cathy, got her period, she and her husband and younger daughter gave Cathy gifts and took her out to dinner. Carla, the younger daughter, is waiting for her celebration.

Carla's friend, Pattie, heard about celebrating your period and said, "It sure beats getting a bottle of aspirin thrown at you." That's what happened to her when she told her parents she had her first period.

Unfortunately, menstruation is often treated as if it's a problem, something to be embarrassed about or ashamed of — as if it's taboo and a secret — for no reason except that it only happens to females. Sometimes a girl learns about menstruation from another girl. That's how I learned: my cousin, who is six months older than I am, told me all about it when she got her period, and when I told my mother, she gave me a booklet to read that was written by a company that makes sanitary napkins. Most girls are shocked when I explain that a

"She has many child-rearing years ahead of her. She represents the future and the spirit."
—Shaniqua

period stops for women around my age — in our late forties and early fifties — during what's called *menopause.* Our periods don't last our whole lives; they only happen during the years we can have a baby if we want to.

Now you have another chance to read out loud. This time it's from a novel called *Brown Girl, Brownstones* by Paule Marshall. In this excerpt, twelve-year-old Selina has strong reactions when her best friend, Beryl, tells her she has her period and that another of their friends, Ina, has hers, too. Selina hasn't gotten her period yet, and she doesn't know what it is even when she's old enough to be menstruating. Many girls have the same experience. I did, too.

They're talking in the park one afternoon, near their homes in Brooklyn, New York. When Beryl tells Selina **"I bleed sometimes,"** Selina's first reaction is to say, **"So what. Everybody does."** Beryl explains that she bleeds

"Not from a cut or anything but from below. Where the baby pops out. Ina does, too. That's why she gets pains every once in a while. I'll tell you, if you want to hear . . ."

"Tell me." And beneath [Selina's] eagerness there was dread.

Beryl raised up, gathering her dress neatly under her. Her eyes flitted nervously across Selina's intense face. Then, with her head bowed and a squeamish look she explained it all. "That's why I'm getting these things," she concluded, jabbing her small breasts. "It happens to all girls."

Selina stared very quietly at her and, for that moment, she was quiet inside, her whole self suspended in disbelief. Then an inexplicable revulsion gripped her and her face screwed with disgust. "It's never going to happen to me," she said proudly.

"It'll happen. It hurts sometimes and it makes you miserable in the summer . . . "

"Well, if it ever happens to me nobody'll ever know. They'll see me change and think it's magic."

"Besides, it makes you feel important."

"How could anyone walking around dripping blood feel important?"

"It's funny but you do. Almost as if you were grown up. It's like . . . oh, it's hard to explain to a kid . . . "

"Who's a kid?"

"You, because you haven't started yet."

"I'll never start!" And beneath her violent denial there was despair.

"Oh yes, you'll start." Beryl nodded wisely. "Wait, lemme try to explain how it makes you feel. The first time I was scared. Then I began to feel different. That's it. Even though nothing's changed and I still play kid games and go around with kids, even though my best friend's a kid" — she bowed to Selina — "I feel different. Like I'm carrying something secret and special inside . . . ."

Selina says she's "still trapped within a hard flat body." She closed her eyes to hide the tears and was safe momentarily from Beryl and Ina and all the others joined against her in their cult of blood and breasts.

After a time Beryl came and lay close to her. She placed her arm comfortingly around her. "What was that poem you wrote about the sky?" she asked. And always her voice calmed Selina. Her disappointment, her anguish tapered slowly until finally her tears were gone and she turned to Beryl and held her . . . . "It wasn't about this kind of sky," she said and began to recite, her thin voice striking the rock and veering off into the sky, her eyes closed, her face serene in sleep. Whispering, Selina recited then to the rock, to the dome of sky, to the light wind, all the poems she had scribbled in class, that came bright and vivid at night.

Beryl stirred in her sleep and pressed Selina closer. Just then the sun rose above the rock. The strong light seemed to smooth the grass, to set the earth steaming richly. They were all joined it seemed: Beryl with the blood bursting each month inside her, the sun, the seared grass and earth — even she, though barren of breasts, was part of the mosaic.

How do you feel about getting your period? How did you learn about your period? You might write in your notebook about your reactions to Selina and Beryl's conversation. Or write your feelings about getting your period in your notebook. Maybe you have a friend who also wants to write about menstruation or menopause.

When Selina is looking up at the sky, I think she has a lot of different feelings all at once. Maybe Lucy felt the same way. Without written words from Lucy's era to tell us how she felt about getting her period, we can imagine what she felt. That's another reason it's important for you to think of history as females having similar experiences. Did Lucy feel left out, the way Selina did at first, or did she welcome it?

We can imagine almost anything, for instance, the very different way we might feel if we knew there is something exciting and powerful about being a female. You might feel differently about female genitals, too, if we didn't live in a culture that often makes them seem dirty or shameful. Just think about the slang words for this magical part of the body. Gloria and I have been trying to think of a new name for female genitals because so many of the names sound bad or weak. We thought about *power bundle.* Maybe you, too, have some suggestions.

The idea that it's special to be female is not new. In researching prehistory, I traveled back in time to almost two hundred thousand years ago.

I discovered that many more images of females have been found than of males. Artifacts or objects from prehistory are mostly of women because of a woman's magical power of gestation, birth, and generating food from her body. For instance, two hundred thousand years ago, a child's grave was covered by a slab of stone. Carved on the underside of the stone, facing the child's body, are pairs of breasts. These carvings are a way of protecting the child. Breast-shaped carvings as images of power are found throughout prehistory.

The first human artifacts I've found copies of that we can hold in our hands are from thirty-seven thousand years ago. They're of female human beings and they're believed to be guardians of the earth. They have no feet and they were stuck upright in the ground. You can see what they looked like in the illustrations in this book. These small statues were used to remind people of the mysterious power of the female to create and care for life on earth.

I wasn't surprised, just disappointed, when I read in a popular book on prehistory that even though most early artifacts are of women, only a picture of a male artifact was included in the book. It made me want to have something even better than pictures to tell us about prehistory. Wouldn't it be great if we could see, feel, and touch exact copies of a lot of early female artifacts?

I decided to collect copies of artifacts of girls and women from prehistory. I wanted the collection to include figures from all seven continents. Then we could hold and touch them and decide for ourselves what other possibilities there are for female human beings.

The artifacts I collected can't talk, of course, but we can see them in "Girls Speak Out." We can be sure they're no longer lost voices because we share our voices with them.

In "Girls Speak Out" sessions, it's a special moment when the artifacts are placed in the center of the circle and we see them together for the first time. Look at the drawings of the artifacts in this book: How do you feel about how different female bodies can look? Some are thin, some are fat, some have big breasts and/or big behinds, and some are small all over. Some of the artifacts

"I am a symbol of other women."
—Tabathea

are made of clay, some are wood, and some are painted with bright colors while others are carved from stone.

One woman said that it was "important to see that the artifacts came in different sizes and shapes and that there was a beauty to each of them." She said she is now "more conscious of being more accepting of how I look and I think we need to be loyal to one another regardless of what we look like."

We give voices to the artifacts by writing what we think and feel about them. Girls have all kinds of ideas about the artifacts' history. When you read what they've written, they may inspire you.

Girls in "Girls Speak Out" groups write by themselves or with other girls. There can be a woman in the group. You may find an artifact you like and write a story about her.

Search in these pages for the artifact that's most interesting to you. Try to imagine what history she's holding inside her that you can set free.

Nine-year-old Leah thinks, "There's a lot more imagining for us to do here because it's not written down."

Words written in "handwriting" like this are the actual words written by girls and women. You can decide to share your artifact story or keep it private. Reading the story aloud is voluntary; girls who enjoy being in front of a group often have someone hold their artifact and they talk to her as well as about her. Some girls want their story printed in the book I put together, but they don't want it read out loud.

One nine-year-old girl, Ruth, confided to an older girl that she couldn't read or write so the older girl wrote the story down. Then Ruth read it out loud, word by word, with our help. Ruth had trouble reading and writing because she wasn't taught at home and she didn't go to school often — the adults in her house didn't care about school, so it was hard for her to get up and be ready with clean clothes in time for the school bus. A group of girls around her age looked out for her and made sure she got to "Girls Speak Out." Being there helped her to know that not going to school wasn't her fault, and didn't mean she couldn't use her intelligence.

Another girl who was eleven told me her artifact story was going to be hard for me to understand because she had a learning problem. She's dyslexic, and she's uncomfortable asking for help. But after she told me her difficulties with writing, she dictated the story to me.

Some girls had the opposite problem — they were so good in school that they only knew how to learn what other people had done, not to use their imagination. They had an easy time reading and writing, but took longer to reach inside themselves.

As you read these stories about the artifacts, remember you can add your story to this collection, too. It's exciting to give the artifacts a voice. You might use pictures instead of words to express what you think an artifact would say.

I think you'll like the girls' names and the names some of them give to the artifacts. Some girls and women called the little statues by their own names, some made up names, and others felt they didn't need names, but each said what females might say if there was the power to say what was really felt by them.

A Young Girl with Four Arms
by Latoya, 10

Once upon a time
I was a little young girl
with four arms and
I was holding the sun
to help my people see better
and be black like me.
And I will make clothes
for my people and
jewelry and bracelets.
They will be gold bracelets
and some silver

but I will feed my people
and I will give them a wish.
And I will make some coats
for raining and boats for snowing
and give them combs and brushes
to do their ponytails
and give them
crowns to make them
kings and queens.

"Tabathea"
by Tabetha, 15

My name is Tabathea. I am special. I don't have to wear clothes because no one else wears clothes. I am a symbol of other women. I walk and talk just as you do, but I do not wear the clothes that you do, but I go undressed because I'm comfortable just as you are in your clothes. I live from day to day as the same.

The only thing that's different is the animals I eat to get nourishment. The symbol I hold in my hand is to call on whichever animal I choose to eat. I am overweight, but it does not bother me because you do not have to live in my body. I'm very comfortable with the way I look. I had many children which is most of the reason I am this way. But you women in this day and age are very tuned into the way you dress and the way you look, but there's no difference between you and I because we are both women.

Back Off
by Toni, 13

Back off. Leave me alone. I can't believe what you punks did to me. You thought I was nothing, but you were wrong. Yes, I'm back, you bully, and mad as heck. I cried and screamed giving birth to your children. You just threw me in a hole with no history, excuse me, herstory. I hope you fear me.

I fed you, clothed you, and took care of you. This is the thanks I get. You are a creature me and my sisters made. You are a man. I loved and respected you, but you dissed me. I am coming to your house and I'm going to stretch myself, play cards with the fellas and have you wait on me hand and foot. But it's not going to happen because you made me without a mouth. That's because you fear me. Then I must have power. My sisters will find you men and diss you, my brother.

Destiny
by Brazley Daraja, 13

Her name is Destiny. She's totally naked, but not embarrassed about it. Her hands are sitting on her large beautiful breasts to draw attention to her body. Also, Destiny has no face because she doesn't need one. Even without a face, even without a mouth, you can still hear her roar. Destiny is proud and powerful. She represents all women because we are all different, but all the same.

My Artifact
by Teneil, 9

My artifact, I believe, is an African queen. She believes that all people are no different. They may be richer, poorer, but she keeps her faith and her beliefs. She keeps strong and when she wants something done, she tries, does not give up. She tries not to fail. A woman is no greater than a man, but we have the power to give life. Women have the dream about things they could never talk about with a man.

Every woman has a gift to give. Women, black or white, could talk together and talk about children and different things. No woman should be afraid of a man because we have a great power men do not have. That's what I feel about being a woman.

My Lost Girl
by Lizard, 11

I am a young girl of long ago. I live in a time when no one had heard of sexism. Men and women are equal in everything they do. I can express my feelings in any way I want to. If I am really excited they do not tell me to calm down. I'm trapped inside a young girl of today. I cannot let out my feelings. No one even knows I exist. I feel like I am dead. For only dead people should not be free.

That is their bodies that are limp while their spirits dance and play in the air. Please set me free to be who I am and what I want to be. Don't keep me trapped. Only here for the public's eye, not for myself. Let me dance and play in the wind and rain. Let me love my friends and cherish nature. If I should kiss a snail, don't have people laugh at me and say how disgusting I am.

I am myself, not another person's property, so I'll let my feelings out so much, and really cry and laugh and do anything that I want to do. I miss the world, the happiness, and the joy that I once had. Get me free through your laughter and your tears, and don't be afraid to show your love to another person. No matter what other people think of them. Let me free!

Los de madera son de Africa
by Monzerrat, 10

Los de madera son de Africa. Y los de madera siempre se peliában el uno con el otro. Y una día uno se escapó y los otros estaban riéndose, pero el se cayó empieza llorar y los otros que estaban riéndose se cayeron también. Y el que se cayó primero estaba riéndose y como vivien juntos se separaron cada uno y comían juntos pero no dormían juntos. Y juguban y mataban animales para comer, como bufalos, peces o venado y comían maíz y otras cosas diferentes. Y el cuero de los bufalos o venado lo usaban para ropa y cosas diferentes como zapátos y dibujos. Lo estiriban para pintar y con la fruta hacían pintura, con naranja y frutos. Y cuando otras personas illegáron les ensenáron a plantar y a los niños les ensenáron juegos y cosas nuevas y a plantar cosas nuevas.

Translation: The Wooden Ones from Africa
by Monzerrat, 10

The wooden ones are from Africa. And they often fought one another. And one day one escaped from the others. They were laughing, but the one that fell down began to cry and the ones that were laughing fell down, too. And the one that fell first was laughing, and since they lived together, they separated and ate together. But they didn't sleep together. And they played and killed animals to eat like buffaloes, fish and deer. And they ate corn and other things and used the hide for clothing and things like shoes and drawings. They stretched it to paint on and with oranges and fruit they made paint. And when other people came, they showed them how to plant and they showed the children games and new things and how to plant things.

Sacred Body
by Tiffany, 26

She wraps her arms tightly around her body because her body is sacred to her. She is able to do things that no man can — the most important, being able to bring new life into this world. She looks into the sky and thinks to herself that the world can be a better place for her and her children if we work together.

The Old Day
by Shamika, 9

This woman's name is Kauo. Kauo is an old woman. She's about 20,000 years old. She's a strong woman because she has a snake on her head and she's holding a globe. She uses her power by rubbing her globe. When she holds her globe, she limps over.

During the day, she feeds her snake. She wears a long dress, a big necklace and she wears her hair in a ponytail. Kauo lives by herself. She lives in Africa. Kavo is a mean lady. She's the meanest lady in Africa.

Two-Spirited Goddess
by Mary, 43

This is the two-spirited goddess of fertility. Her name is Frog Woman. Two-Spirited: she is woman and man. She claims a woman's power to bring forth life. The village prays to Frog Woman for rain. Rain means life for the village. It means food to make the body strong to bring forth life.

Frog Woman tells women to take control of our bodies. She tells us to be self-assured and confident in our power. She tells us to love our bodies and the source of our power.

Grandmother
by Serinna, 12

Once upon a time there was a group of women. They would catch fish all day so they could eat. The biggest woman gets to be the queen because she was the warmest and the safest.

But one day she fell asleep, and they couldn't wake her up. Then they got a bell and she woke up. The ladies told her they were going for a swim. Grandmother was asleep again and it was even harder to wake her up. They rang the bell for a longer time than they did before, and it finally woke her up.

Each time grandmother fell asleep it was harder to wake her up. When she fell asleep, everybody would all lay around her and restore her warmth. And they would sing her awake.

Tamer of Horses
by Joanna, 9

While each part of my body was being carved into the wall, I felt happy because I felt like I was coming to life, but when I was taken out it felt like I was being killed.

The horses are my companions. They are the only ones who understand me. I am the only one who understands them.

First I was carved because I was the first ever to communicate with horses. The horses are my friends, but they were also the first horses ever to like a human. From then on horses were known as carefree and happy.

I've got a message for all you people out there: Girls are as good as boys and girls can do the same things.

I know because everyone teased me about trying to tame horses, but now everyone is thanking me for absolutely everything.

My life ended peacefully, burned and buried.

Saferia
by Abigail, 15

"Saferia": (sah-fear-ah) one of strength, essence and beauty.

Saferia was one of the beauties in a relatively small town in India. Everything about her represents alot of what she is, but can be easily misread, like most women today.

Saferia was created with darkly outlined eyes to emphasize or more likely to symbolize the windows to her soul. The more you look into them and try to understand them and what they try to say, the more bewildered and interested you are in knowing how to decipher the language and answer in the same way.

Her long hair represents her beauty, and yet adds to her strength and mystery. It gives her a sexuality all her own. Her feline ways are expressed through the cat on her head. She is agile, witty, curious, intelligent, quick, and always lands on her feet.

Her face displays her willingness to love only those who are deserving.

Her figure and breasts serve as a temporary holding place for a carefree, loving, and insatiable spirit. Her spirit is trapped inside looking for its counterpart to set her free.

Her beauty is where her strength is because it's natural. It's not doctored or created, but enhanced by her soul. What is natural is undeniable and unstoppable. When something cannot be stopped, it is strong.

Her beauty also serves as a defense. It protects her from the ugliness around her, the nature of man.

Tall, fair and beautiful, with a smile like the sun.
Her hips like songs waiting to be sung.
Her eyes like wounds, full of much pain.
Her lips wet and perfectly round like pellets of rain.
Her hair like roots searching for earth.
Her breasts stand out, ready to give birth,
Give birth to her heart and soul
Her body holds her spirit one and whole.
She is like a story waiting to be told.
Her heart is up for sale, waiting to be sold . . . .

A Spiritual Woman
by Kila, 10

Once upon a time I was a spiritual woman. I was also faithful to my people. I was hurt when people made fun of my spiritual life. My clothes were made of the finest silk in town. I lived all alone in a small house in the village.

In my country, angels walk with women and watch over men.

I was born with the ability to carve in wood. Then I became famous for my beautiful sculptures.

And Angel is my famous name.

Mujer Palo
by Bertha, 12

Ella es de Africa. Ella es grande. No tiene manos pero sí tiene pies y tiene noventa años y es flaquita. Es bonita. Tiene su cara pintada. Tiene cuello grande es una mujer fuerte. La pintura representa algo, un símbolo de mujer grande y fuerte.

Translation: Woman of Wood
by Bertha, 12

She's from Africa. She is big. She doesn't have hands, but she does have feet and she's ninety years old and is thin. She's pretty. She has a painted face. She has a big neck and is a strong woman. The paint represents something, a symbol of a big and strong woman.

Leila
by Nypri, 11

Once, long ago, there lived a woman who people thought was very strange. She did everything backwards. She would dress up in raggedy clothes and go to important places and people would look at her funny because they were wearing fancy clothes and she was wearing raggedy clothes. She would also hide her face.

But every night at midnight, she would gather all her horses and go in the fields with fancy instead of raggedy clothes and gather stones in a circle and make a fire in the middle of the rocks with leaves in her hair and start dancing with horses.

But she would dance on rocks. It would make her feet stronger and her more powerful. She would celebrate herself because she was happy. That's one reason why people thought she was strange. P.S. This story took place in Ethiopia.

Cleopatra's Baby
by Lydia, 9

Hi, I'm Cleopatra's baby.

When I was found with my family many years later, I was parted from all but two of my family. I cried when they were taken away for I'm only six months old. But luckily, I managed to take two of the magic coins they dug up. My mother had told me about them before we were buried thousands of years before! And that if I ever saw them to grab as many as I could.

Since they're as tall as I, I could only get two, the Earth and the Sky, the two most powerful of them all. The Earth 'cause the most living things are on it, and the Sky because the Moon and Sun are in it. So I grabbed them and it made me stay the same age forever. And gave me all the power of the earth and sky. I then grew big and am the most powerful Sorceress in the world.

That's all I have to say till another thousands of years pass and I have more to say.

Arama (Meaning Spirit of Life)
by Shaniqua, 16

This artifact is very open. She shows naiveté and sweetness. I think she is young. She is at the age where her breasts are budding and her pelvis and hips are coming out. She has many child-bearing years ahead of her.

She represents the future and the spirit of her village.

Since she's so open and honest, she probably knows everyone else's problems. She does have a mischievous side. The fact that her feet are pointy suggests she does not work on hard tasks, it shows her femininity and daintiness.

Her arms are stretched out in a surrendering gesture. It shows she's pure, innocent, and free. She isn't restrained. I believe she's seen much, but hasn't been deeply affected by the trials of her village life. Her posture shows she's been thoroughly molded by her childhood.

What makes her who she is living day by day. She makes the best of her days and wants to be different without being strange or outcast. She wants to follow and live a normal village life, yet she also wants to experience life as a whole.

I feel she's a virgin who has been untouched because her legs were made stuck together. Boys have probably tried to get to her, but she held fast. She was considered very beautiful in her tribe. Not only because of her face, but her inner strength and life. Her mother is proud of her, but prays daily that she might make the right choices.

Her complexion is black, but oddly mixed with her red and brown side. This can show she has many sides or is interested in many things. I'm sure she's been the center of attention many times. She has a wiseness beyond her young years. She will grow old happy. She is one of the prospect youngsters of the village.

She gives her village life, and gives her nationality color and her country spirit. She will be remembered many years after her death, because she is the Arama spirit of life.

The Story of My Artifact
by Lizzy, 10

I'm going to call my "model" woman, Sarabi. Here is the story she tells.

I was born in Africa. My mother took care of all the people in the town. She was what you would call a medicine woman. I was born in a hut, on the plain, by the Great River. I was very sick when I was born. My mother took care of me until I was well. My mother had gotten the disease that I had had. Unfortunately, since she did not have the strength to speak and tell Mistress what to do, my mother died.

So I went and lived with Mistress, who was the "queen" of the village.

My sickness had left me, not deformed, but in a way, different. I could tell things that other people could not. I understood things about the world no one had ever dreamed of. Maybe it was the medicine Mother had given me, but something about me was different, special.

One day, I asked Mistress, "What is more than the Great Number?"

She said to me, "There is NOTHING more than the Great Number, ten, and that is why it is so Great!"

I pondered it, but I did not understand it. There's always something more of something.

I went outside and got ten of the gray rocks from the ground. I thought to myself, I can get more than that. So I picked up another rock and put it with the others. See, there is one more than the Great Number.

I did not tell Mistress about my discovery because I thought she might be angry at me for defying the Great Number.

I was almost a grown woman. Tomorrow I would be as old as the Great Number. I had already had my first and second child. Both girls, wonders of nature.

I was the medicine woman of my village. Many had died from the terrible disease, Cuptum. I had many to treat. There were many I could do nothing for. I got the disease.

I would not let my children near me. I did not want them to get sick.

I died one of your "months" after I caught the disease. I felt proud of myself, because I had worked as hard as I could to discover new things that needed discovering. That is why my arms are in such a position.

Remember. Bring everyone into you, to help them, and use your given knowledge to discover what needs discovering.

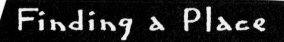

Finding a Place

We can give these artifacts homes, too. Imagine the floor of the room you're in is covered with cutouts of the seven continents so it looks like a giant map or a flattened globe. In a "Girls Speak Out" session, large continents made from green fabric are spread on the floor. I ask the girls to place their artifact on the continent where they think she would feel most at home. Then the girls and women are asked to choose a continent to sit on where *they* feel most at home: it can be where they live, where they're descended from, or where they would like to visit or live.

Which continent would you choose? How much do you know about the country or continent your ancestors come from? When a Chinese-American woman sat on the Asian continent, she was surprised to discover that the girl sitting next to her was Japanese-American. They had known each other before and not talked about their ancestry. There's a mix of different races, cultures, and ages on each continent when everyone is seated that's similar to how it is on the actual continents.

Girls of African descent may come from different continents and islands and so may others in this world where people move around — sometimes by choice and sometimes not. We often talk about how some of the girls' ancestors were stolen from Africa and how, if they survived the journey, they were sold as slaves here and in other countries. During "Girls Speak Out" in Chicago, girls talked about what they were studying in black history in Girl Scouts and the YWCA. They told me they believe the white people they know today are not responsible for the slave trade, but wondered what people had learned about racism from at least the last two hundred years of history.

One female ex-slave who tried to educate people about racism, sexism, and classism had the name So-journer Truth. The name Isabella was given to her at birth in 1797 and her last name changed with each new master. She was freed after thirty years as a slave, and in 1843 changed her name to show the woman she had become: a traveler on a journey who was telling the truth about her experiences as a woman and as a slave. Her audiences weren't used to hearing women speak, especially a black woman who was a feminist, but So-

"Today I feel I could take on the world."
—Elizabeth

journer was a tall, strong woman and a magical speaker who commanded attention.

She was spiritual and would also sing songs about her feelings and experiences as if she were in a different kind of church. She joined with the abolitionists, a movement of people who wanted to get rid of slavery. It was also unusual for a woman to talk about and be active in politics, since women of all races and black men were forbidden to vote and, in many states, even to speak in public.

If you could change your name to show who you are or what you want to do, what new name would you choose? Would you keep all or part of your name?

One black feminist who's a writer today changed her name to her great-grandmother's name. Instead of Gloria Watkins she became bell hooks because her great-grandmother "talked back" and bell wants to do the same thing to racism and the patriarchy. bell also uses lowercase letters in her name to indicate that a person's name is not more important than other words. She prefers to use "white supremacy" instead of "racism" since the second could be people of color who consider themselves superior, too. And white supremacy describes what is really happening.

Is there anyone you admire whose name you would adopt? With or without a new name, would you be a speaker, a singer, and/or a writer? Would you like to be a political activist like Sojourner?

Tara is a nine-year-old girl in New York, where Sojourner was born, and during a "Girls Speak Out" session she asked why there has never been a woman president of the United States. We explained about many women being persuaded that their vote didn't count even after they won the legal right to vote. We talked about how a patriarchy makes it hard for a woman to be president because we aren't allowed to take the steps to get there or to have the money to run for office. But we said that in the last hundred years or so, a woman's movement has been helping females to become powerful. Tara carefully listened to our explanations. Then she said, "I'm going to be the first one."

Sojourner was one of the first women political activists even though she couldn't read or write. Another female abolitionist, Frances Dana Gage, wrote what Sojourner said just the way she said it in what's called "dialect," or folkspeech, which is the way a particular person really sounds as opposed to what is on the page. This is what Frances wrote as the opening lines of one of Sojourner's most famous speeches:

"Wall, chilren, what dar is so much racket dar must be somethin out o kilter.... But what's all dis here talkin bout? Dat man ober dar say dat womin needs to be helped into carriages, and lifted ober ditches, and to hab de best place everywhar."

You can read the rest of this speech in folkspeech in *Black Women in America: An Historical Encyclopedia.*

Patricia C. McKissack and Fredrick McKissack wrote a biography called *Sojourner Truth: Ain't I a Woman?* The title comes from the speech I quoted above in which, among other things, Sojourner challenges the audience to remember that slave women and poor women showed that women were not too weak or ladylike to be equal, what some anti-abolitionist men were trying to say about women in general. The meeting where Sojourner first asked the question "Ain't I a Woman?" took place in a church in Akron, Ohio, where the Woman's Rights Convention of 1851 was being held.

When Sojourner begins to speak, the crowd is angry. (The McKissacks reprint the speech in standard English.)

"Well, children, where there is so much racket, there must be somethin' out of kilter. . . . The white men will be in a fix pretty soon. But what's all this about anyway?

"That man over there," she said pointing to a minister who had said a woman's place was to be a mother, wife and companion, good sister and loving niece. Among other things he also said women were the "weaker sex."

To this Sojourner took issue. "He says women need to be helped into carriages and lifted over ditches and to have the best everywhere. Nobody ever helps me into carriages, over mud puddles, or gets me any best places."

And raising herself to her full height, she asked, "And ain't I a woman?"

Sojourner turned to the men who were seated behind her. "Look at me!" She bared her right arm and raised it in the air. The audience gasped as one voice. Her dark arm was muscular, made strong by hard work. "I have ploughed. And I have planted." No doubt she was remembering the years she had worked. . . to earn early freedom. "And I have gathered into barns. And no man could head me." She paused again and asked this time in a whisper. "And ain't I a woman?"

"I have borne [thirteen] children and seen them sold into slavery, and when I cried out in a mother's grief, none heard me but Jesus. And ain't I a woman?" [No doubt Sojourner was thinking about her mother but used "I" instead. Sojourner only had five children.]

Then one by one she took on the male religious pedants. "You say Jesus was a man so that means God favors men over women. Where did your Christ come

from?" She asked again. "Where did he come from?"
Then she answered her own question. "From God and
a woman. Man had nothing to do with him."

She challenged the widely held belief that women
were less intelligent than men, and blacks had no intel-
lect at all. "Suppose a man's mind holds a quart, and
woman's don't hold but a pint; if her pint is full, it's
as good as a quart." Her common sense ripped at the
core of male hypocrisy.

Sojourner directed her conclusion to the women in
the audience. "If the first woman God ever made was
strong enough to turn the world upside down all
alone, these women together ought to be able to turn
it back and get it right-side up again and now that they
are asking to do it, the men better let 'em." . . . .

Sojourner's "truth" was simple. Racism and sexism
were unacceptable to people of good reason.

Thinking about how Sojourner tried to change the
patriarchal, racist system may give you some ideas about
what you'd change today to make life fair for children
you know. Remember, Sojourner took a lot of chances
and said and did a lot of risky things in her lifetime.

Sojourner once told a friend, "I have two skins. I
have a white skin under and a black one to cover it."
Using this idea that each of us is universal, what kind of
artifact would you design for her?

In "Girls Speak Out," girls make their own artifacts with clay or they draw them, but these artifacts are not of someone from the past. As a matter of fact, they move us into the present, even into the future, because they're about each girl in "Girls Speak Out," including you.

What kind of artifact would you make to show who you are? Girls have created many things: crowns, a soccer ball being held on fingertips, a young girl sitting with the planet in her lap, an infinity symbol, and a book with a pen holder. You can draw your artifact in your notebook, you can make a collage that expresses how you feel about who you are, or you can use clay. You may have your own idea about how to create an artifact.

Sometimes a girl asks us to guess what her artifact says about her. What could we guess about you? Is there someone you know who you wish knew more about you? Maybe you can ask her or him to guess what your artifact says about you and that will help her or him to understand you better.

Making Choices

While the girls are working on their original artifacts, I ask them if they have any questions for each other and/or for the women in the room.

Is there anything you want to know about growing up? Are there things older girls or women do that excite or puzzle you? Asking questions can clear up a lot of things and help you decide what you want for your own future.

If you write your questions in your notebook, you might find you have some of the same issues on your mind as the girls I've met — or you may put something into words that other girls are interested in, too.

Judy's a nine-year-old girl in New York City and she asked the women in the group when they had children. She looked surprised as each woman answered her. One by one, we explained our different experiences: I was twenty-six when I had my son; the Haitian woman next to me had two daughters before she was twenty-five; a woman from North Carolina said she decided not to have children and she was forty-five; another woman became a mother at thirty-three, and one twenty-one-year-old woman said she wanted to have children later on in life, if at all.

Judy then asked why we did or didn't have children. I said I became pregnant soon after I had cancer and I wanted to have the baby because it was a life-affirming event. The Haitian woman said she wanted daughters and was glad when they were born close together so they could keep each other company because she herself had been lonely as a child. The woman who didn't choose to have children said she had an interesting life without children. The remaining two women talked about waiting to share their lives until they felt comfortable taking care of someone for a lifetime.

A young woman asked Judy if she was interested in having children. Judy told us her three sisters, who were sixteen, eighteen, and nineteen, had children and they lived at home with the babies. She didn't think she wanted children and she couldn't figure out two things: How to have a family if you didn't have kids and how to belong to the "circle of life" if you didn't give birth.

One woman talked about having a family of friends she chose to be with as well as with her children and husband. Two of the women were single parents like me, and we said we thought of ourselves as families. I even think of myself as a "double parent" because I raised my son without his father's help. The woman with no birth children said she had a lot of friends and nieces and nephews who were part of her family. My friend Gloria is in her sixties and she's surrounded by young women who are like daughters even though she didn't give birth to children. I have friendships with more and more girls and young women as I get older and I feel like I have daughters as well as a son.

When I asked Judy why she thought she had to give birth to belong to the circle of life, she talked about the movie, *The Lion King,* in which there's a song about a circle of life. Judy said she thought having babies was the only way for females to belong to the human race even though she didn't think that was true for boys or men. In the movie, the lion cub's mother is very briefly on screen and it's because she's given birth to the new lion king. "She's not a lion queen, either," said another girl. Later in the session, Judy said she felt better having more choices to think about.

A girl in Portland, Oregon, asked how old girls and women were when they became interested in boys as boyfriends. One seventeen-year-old girl said she had a boyfriend for the last few months. They talked on the phone a lot and went out to the movies and to friends' houses, but she felt it was no big deal because she had

"Bring everyone into you, to help them, and use your given knowledge to discover what needs discovering."
—Lizzy

other things to do. She wanted to be a writer and getting married wasn't on her mind yet.

When a sixteen-year-old girl said she really, really wanted a boyfriend, another girl her age said that girls with boyfriends aren't always as happy as you imagine them to be when you don't have one. She said she had a steady boyfriend at sixteen, but she wanted more time to herself because she wasn't able to be by herself enough. She felt pressure to be a girlfriend from her boyfriend, and from the girls she knew.

One of the young women there was getting married in two weeks. She said that she had been friends with boys when she was a teenager. She thought she had a good relationship with her fiancé because they were also each other's best friends.

When a sixteen-year-old girl named Jane said she wasn't interested in boys, some of the other girls said they had felt like that, but their feelings had changed. When Jane insisted she liked hanging out with girls better, they tried to convince her that she would change, too. Then a twelve-year-old girl, Kate, spoke about feeling "different" from girls who talked about boys all the time and how they wanted a boyfriend in a romantic way.

Tina, who's thirteen and lives in Harlem, a big African-American community in New York City, said her aunt was a nurse. Tina's aunt explained to Tina that during puberty she would experience many different feelings. Tina told the girls in the session that "I could be interested in boys. I could be interested in girls. I could be bisexual and interested in both sexes. Who knows? I'm going to be open-minded about it."

Tina said she feels "connected to everyone and everything on the planet." She knows some kids and grown-ups are upset by bisexuality and homosexuality, but she thinks what people do with their sex life is "none of my business. I just have to figure out who I am."

What parents expect of girls in school was an issue that led fifteen-year-old Cassie to ask the older women in the group if they were close to their parents and sisters and brothers as grown-ups. She said she felt her parents wanted her to live life for them — to do the things they missed. Cassie was afraid of disappointing them if she does what she wants to do. She told us that even when she was doing something she wanted to — like doing well in school — if her parents wanted the same thing, she was still unhappy. "That's because," she explained, "if they want me to do it and they don't care what I want, it's like I don't count. I need to do it for me. That's who I am, not just who *they* want me to be."

Two young women in San Diego were close in age: they were twenty-three and twenty-five. They looked like sisters, but they weren't related. Roz and Minna said they had a hard time getting along with their mothers who thought they had become "too independent." They weren't interested in marriage and they both had careers they liked — they worked with teenagers in high schools — but they didn't earn a lot of money.

Roz and Minna lived with roommates and enjoyed living away from their parents' homes. Each hoped she would get along better with her mother as she got older. They thought part of their problem was they came from cultures — Mexican and Filipino — that often said women should marry young, have children, and give up everything else.

A sixteen year old said she couldn't even mention moving out of the house to her parents. She wanted to travel for a year after high school, but her parents would explode whenever she tried to bring it up. Other girls said they had older sisters who didn't do what their parents wanted them to do, so they felt it was their turn to make their parents happy. Some girls said they were the oldest or the only child; they felt responsible for fulfilling everyone else's expectations in order to be a successful adult.

Roberta is a young woman who was an only child, and she told us her mother encouraged her to do what she liked to do. Her mother was a single parent, and it was hard for her mother to earn enough money to support them and send Roberta away to college. Roberta's mother is a writer now, something she always wanted to be, but she couldn't earn enough money as a writer when Roberta was growing up. Roberta says she still feels free to be who she wants to be.

Girls often talk about how the media makes teenage mothers seem like losers, and they say they're scared of "making the same mistake." I often read from a novel about a seventeen-year-old girl who works in a factory to support her two children. A fourteen-year-old girl who wants to go to college is her baby-sitter.

In *Make Lemonade,* by Virginia Euwer Wolff, when fourteen-year-old LaVaughn sees a note that says BABYSITTER NEEDED BAD it leads her to Jolly, a teenage mother whose children have different, absent fathers. LaVaughn wants to earn money, but she thinks her mother won't like her spending time with Jolly. I'm including the part where LaVaughn explains why she wants to babysit, despite the fact that Jolly lives in

. . .even a worse place than where we live.
The sidewalk is sticky,
the garbage cans don't have lids, somebody without
    teeth
was talking to herself in front of the door.

Because the novel is written as if it was poetry, it looks and often sounds like it has the rhythm of speech. It's easy to read aloud. I encourage you to read aloud, too.

This word COLLEGE is in my house,
and you have to walk around it in the rooms
like furniture.
Here's the actual conversation
way back when I'm in 5th grade
and my Mom didn't even have her gray hairs yet.
I'm sitting on the high stool in the kitchen
cutting up carrots and celery. You have to understand
this vegetable work would be a big deal for a little kid
which I was one then.
My Mom was putting the other stew things
together in the pot
and I was thinking about the movie they showed in
   school.

It was about how you go to college
and the whole place is clean with grass planted
and they have lion statues and flowers growing.
You study in books and do science in a lab with
   microscopes
and you get to live in the dormitory and make
   popcorn.
Then you graduate
and you wear a cap and gown and it's outdoors.
Then you get a good job and you live in a nice place
with no gangs writing all over the walls.

I just up and asked her while we doing the stew.
"Can I go to college when I'm big?"
My Mom turns her whole body to look at me
and she stops with the stewpot
and after she looks for a while she says,
"Nobody in this building" —
she waves her arms out sideways with the wooden
    spoon —
"ever went to college, nobody in my family,"
and she pulling her chin up
and her shoulders and her chest, and she says,
no breath in between,
"somebody got to be the first, right?" And she goes
    back
to the stew.

Nobody in the building? It has 64 apartments.

I used to count the buzzers while I waited
for the squeaky elevator.
In 64 apartments nobody ever went to college.
She told me very clear, so I never forgot it yet
in all these 4 years since,
"You don't get college easy.
College takes 2 things,
money and hard work. And I don't know what else.
I never got there to find out.

Mostly you don't quit what you start.
You stick to the work you begin. You hear me,
    LaVaughn?"

I tell her Yes I hear her.
"We don't have college money, LaVaughn. You hear
    me?"
"Yes."
"You have to earn it. You listening to me?"
"Yes." This was brand-new news to me in fifth grade.
And some other time, maybe that night,
maybe another night,
she was saying good night
and have you done your homework,
and she said, "You go to college, you make me prouder
than I been in my whole life.
That's the truth, LaVaughn. I tell you."

And another time, I don't know when,
she says to me, she's blow-drying her hair to go to
    work,
she yells, "Listen here, LaVaughn,
what I said about we don't have college money?
You remember?"
I come around the side and yell up in her face
over the blow-dryer,
"Yeah, I remember."

She goes, "Well, we'll have a little bit. A little bit of it.
You earn it mostly, I can put in a little bit. . . ."

That's why that word COLLEGE is in our house
all the time,
it's why I babysit,
it's why I do all the homework all the time,
it's what will get me out of here.
We don't talk about it every day
but it's there.

An African-American woman from a black community in Kansas told us she grew up seeing black women and men in charge of the businesses in town. Her father owned a gas station. She decided to learn about business, went to college, and graduated with a business degree. She now runs a nationwide program for girls.

Sometimes, though, there's no one in a girl's home who can give her the information she needs. My parents thought going to college "wasn't practical" and that I should get a job and marry after high school. I wasn't happy with that idea, but reading and learning excited me so I found out from my favorite teachers how to apply to local colleges. I thought if I lived at home my parents wouldn't try to stop me. It worked, although I still wanted the choice of going away to school or living at home. Sometimes you can't do something you want, so you choose the main thing.

A forty-eight-year-old woman told us that when she was eight or nine she used to go to the library every day after school in the Bronx, New York, because there were no books in her home to read. She would stay until the library closed.

One day, the librarian asked her if she wanted to take the books home and the girl was shocked. She didn't know that you could take library books into your house. Now she's a literature teacher.

Gloria, who's a writer, found the books she read as a girl in her garage. Her father used to buy people's books at auctions after they had died. He would sell the valuable books, and put the rest in the garage. She was also taking care of her sick mother, and not going to school, so she went out to the garage and picked up the first book she found. She loved reading and she learned a lot. Now she thinks that because no one told her what she was supposed to read, she learned early to think for herself. No one told her that *Gone With the Wind* was for grown-ups, so she read it when she was eight.

In *Make Lemonade,* LaVaughn doesn't tell her mother that Jolly's only seventeen because she knows her mom thinks teenage mothers are bad influences — and LaVaughn feels that way, too. As LaVaughn gets to know

Jolly and her kids, Jeremy and Jill, however, her ideas about how Jolly got into her situation change:

I heard somebody say Jolly didn't face reality.
Jolly she says, "You say that?
Reality is I got baby puke on my sweater & shoes
and they tell me they'll cut off the electricity
and my kids would have to take a bath in cold water.
And the rent ain't paid like usual.
Reality is my babies only got one thing in the whole
    world and that's me and that's the reality.
You say I don't face reality? You say that?"

One day LaVaughn gets angry at Jolly because there are no clean clothes for two-year-old Jeremy. LaVaughn says

"That's the way you did the birth control too?
Part way is good enough?"

Jolly answers

"You carry your schoolbooks
like they're some kind of Bibles,
you go to your classes, you pass your tests,
you smile all pretty at your teachers,
is that gonna make you never get pregnant
some guy gets you down where he wants you?"

Although their friendship is difficult, LaVaughn continues to babysit when Jolly goes back to school. Near
the end of the book, Jolly tells LaVaughn a story she
heard at school. It's about a blind woman who buys an
orange for her hungry kids. On her way home, some
boys trip her and they switch a lemon for the orange.
She doesn't realize what they've done and she thanks
the boys for helping her. LaVaughn says the woman
should have figured it was a lemon, and at least **"felt it
careful."**

"That's what they always say," [Jolly] says.
"They always say,
'You should've known you was getting a lemon.'"
She exaggerates her voice.

I begin to get the picture.
"But you don't always know at first," Jolly says.
"You even thank them for it most of the time. See?
See how they get you when you're down,
you don't even know it's a lemon."
She'd building up steam, this Jolly is.
"You even thank them for it,
and you go stumblin' home,
all bleeding or however you're hurt —
and you say to yourself,
    "Well, gosh, I guess somebody give me a lemon.

Ain't I stupid.
Ain't I dumb. I must've deserved it.
if I was so stupid not to know."
And Jolly looks at me,
angry because she understands.

How does the story end? The woman finds "**this lit-tle teensy bit of old caked, lumpy sugar**" and she makes lemonade for her kids.

And I get the point of it this time.

And I want to put my arms all the way around Jolly
in congratulation
and I'm so happy she's so angry
and I'm proud of her
she made it clearer than my Mom ever did
with all the preaching and huffing
and bootstraps.

In Oregon, when I finished reading this selection, nine-year-old Teresa threw her arms up and said, "I'm so happy." Maybe that helped her to understand and/or feel understood, too.

Going into the Woods

Have you ever had experiences that turned out to be the opposite of what you expected? How far back can you remember? What experiences influenced you the most? This could be the beginning of your history of you. You may draw or write about your earliest memories. And you can add more to your life story as you grow up.

Eleven-year-old Sarah thinks magic is a part of her life. She says that there's "something I can feel, maybe it's fairies, maybe not, but there's something special out there I believe in, yes, I do, I believe in magic." A girl asked Sarah if it was like the feeling at holidays, "the spirit of Christmas." When Sarah was talking about whether she believed in magic, even though it was not supposed to be real and/or she was too old to believe in "stuff like that," everyone was laughing along with her and shaking their heads in agreement. It seems we all believe in magic.

Twelve-year-old Bertha said she felt something magical happen when she was walking and thinking on the beach near her home. She started dreaming about being a doctor in Mexico and it made her so happy, she says she "felt it wasn't a dream at all, that it was real." She said she'll remember that moment as magic whenever she thinks about who she is.

You can add your feelings about magic and magical moments to your notebook. Maybe you can describe or draw a moment like that and include it in your history.

Sierra commented that "history is just what happens. When someone writes it down in a book, they write it from their own agenda. Everyone who has written those books has his or her own agenda. And I don't know if there has ever been a time when men didn't have control."

Seventeen-year-old Evelyn reminded us that stories were being told before the patriarchy took over five thousand years ago. She said people tell each other stories all the time and they're stories that have never been written down.

Evelyn is talking about an *oral tradition,* how stories and history had been passed down by talking. There were special people who were storytellers, and they listened, learned and passed the stories down to the next generation — so they just kept going for thousands of years. We asked Evelyn to be the "Girls Speak Out" village storyteller and pretend she knew where each of our mothers was born and something about her life. Can you make up an oral history for yourself? Of course, following an oral tradition means telling it to someone and not reading it, but we remember what we've heard as well as what we've read. Heard or read, we remember stories.

One afternoon, I had a "Girls Speak Out" reunion in a public housing development in New York City. I thought the girls wanted to meet again to come up with a way to keep "Girls Speak Out" going on their own. They did have that expectation, and they soon started what they call "Girls' Studies" twice a month. They talk about women's history, what issues interest them, and sometimes they read books or ask older women to attend, too.

As we talked at the reunion, I realized they also expected me to tell a story, and I hadn't brought any books with me. Luckily, that morning I had been talking with a terrific storyteller, Clarissa Pinkola Estés. Clarissa and I were discussing a story in her book, *Women Who Run with the Wolves,* that I thought would be good to tell the girls.

Clarissa reminded me, "You have *your own stories* to tell." I knew she was right, and so I'm going to tell you one of my stories called "Going into the Woods." I can tell it from memory, almost as if I lived it, but I used some of my experiences and made up the rest. When I was writing it, I felt as if Sequoia, the girl in the story, was telling it to me.

I live near a redwood forest that I walk in almost every day when I'm at home; there's a river running through the middle of my town that floods almost every winter, and it empties into the Pacific Ocean, just a few miles away. The woods, the river and the flood in my story come from my experiences living in Guerneville, California. I imagine there are places and events in your life that would be good ingredients in a story.

I hope the story of Sequoia, who goes into the woods, inspires you to create your own, unique story that you'll tell to someone. The stories we carry inside us, that we create, are as important as the ones we find in books.

Once there was a girl who lived with her people in a place where giant trees grow, trees that are so tall they catch the rain just as it leaves the clouds. It's often very dark where these trees grow because they block the sun, and the girl's people don't go into the woods. They call it "The Dark Place."

The girl's name is Sequoia, she's nine years old, and she lives just a short walk from the dark place. All her life Sequoia wanted to go into the woods. She believed she would be where she wanted most in her life to be, a place where someone would listen to her and know that she had feelings, too. It seemed to her that as hard as they tried, the people she knew, including her parents, just didn't think she was as special as a boy. Inside, Sequoia felt as tall as the trees in the dark place. She knew they were special too, and she felt sad that she couldn't go into the woods.

Each winter, when it rained, sometimes as much as two feet in one day, the river in town would rise up, and come close to the edge of the dark place. Sequoia heard her grandfather say that even the water was afraid to go into the woods. Everyone was quiet when he said that. Sequoia wanted to disagree with him, but she had been told not to say what she was thinking out loud if it would cause trouble. There were a lot of things she didn't say, but she thought often about a moment when she would say what she was thinking about the dark place — and some other things, too, that she had on her mind.

Sequoia was what her mother called a "water baby." She had learned to swim in the river when she was small enough to hold in two hands, and she couldn't remember ever feeling scared of the water. To her it seemed as big and welcoming as the giant trees. It had an everywhere kind of feeling, like the joy she felt sometimes when she watched the sun touch her kitten's head and everything seemed to come together.

During a flood, she watched the river to see how far it would dare to go, breaking all the rules her people set for it.

The winter I'm talking about, it rained two feet in ten hours and it kept on raining. It was Sequoia's birthday, and she spent the day watching the rain fall. She went outside to help her mother dig a ditch where the water could run off away from their house in case the creek behind her house rose so fast that there was what they called a "flash flood." Then the water from behind the house could come up so fast — in a flash — that everything in its way would be swept into the river and carried to the mouth of the river where it empties into the ocean.

There was a flash flood that day, but it was at a friend's house and almost everyone ran to dig ditches. Then they stayed to help clean up and reclaim things of theirs that had been swept into the friend's backyard.

Sequoia stayed at home, and she decided that she would dig a ditch from her bedroom to the dark place. She hoped that the water would rise, take her into the woods, and there she could say everything she wanted to say, out loud, in the place where it was okay to be herself. She dug behind the house, and as the afternoon was turning into night, she realized that she was so strong that she would make it to the edge of the woods and be home in time for the evening meal.

Her parents were coming down the path, covered with silt from the river, and they said they had to go back after getting some food because there were flash floods all over town. It was still raining.

Sequoia wasn't feeling disappointed about missing her birthday celebration because she had plans, too. She promised her parents she would be safe, and they left after throwing together some food and gathering up some dry clothes.

Sequoia's ditches were filling with water. She connected them to the ditch running alongside the path and then she crossed her fingers that so much water would come that she would float into the woods. She was soon rewarded. The water rose quickly and before she could think twice, she was on her way into the woods.

When she finally was able to stand up, she saw she would have been in total darkness if it wasn't for the full moon sneaking here and there among the tree tops. The blackness felt good. And there was something strange happening, too. It wasn't raining under the trees. There was a canopy of branches above her head that shielded her. The trees were covering her. She walked over to one giant tree and felt its bark. It

"Sometimes what people say to me can really mean a lot."
—Adeola

came away in her hands in scratchy pieces and when the moon shone on the bark, she saw it was reddish-brown in color.

"Why, you have red wood," she said to the tree. "Your color is like my skin color. I knew we were from the same place."

Sequoia walked through some of the trees which had holes so big that they were like tunnels. She talked with a jack rabbit and a doe who were playing on the opposite side of the creek. She talked about feeling strong, as strong as anyone she knew, and she told the trees that she was as tall inside as they were outside. They didn't seem to mind. She thought they liked having her company.

When she wandered back to the edge of the woods, she saw she had made a path in the twigs, branches and ferns covering the ground. And she heard voices calling her name.

"They're calling you, too," she said to the tall trees. "We are the same, aren't we? And with you, I see how powerful I am and how powerful everything is. I'm telling my people I'm coming back into the woods. Maybe they'll come, too. No matter what, I'll be back."

Sequoia walked to the edge of the woods, and saw her grandfather who was trembling with anger like a young sapling.

She called to him, "Grandfather, you're wrong about

the woods." She walked up to him and said, in a gentle voice that soothed him, "Maybe some day you'll understand, if you listen to what I have to say. After all, I have been in the dark place and I can tell you what I feel. It's my special place."

Sequoia was right, she did come back to the place she could be herself, sometimes by walking into the redwoods and sometimes by quietly visiting her place inside herself where she was also protected from the rain and safe in the darkness.

Girls are usually quiet after a story, especially one about a young girl going into the woods alone. Lin, a nine-year-old girl, leaned forward in her chair, and I could see she wanted to ask a question. She had been silent during our earlier meetings, and now everyone waited for her to speak.

Lin sat up straight and asked, "Why do we go into the woods?"

I said, "I think it's because in the woods we find joy and sorrow, love, fear and hope — and life. Unless you take a risk, you can't find your strength."

Lin thought for a moment and then she said, "Oh, I didn't know that, but that's it, that's what life is about."

A month later, Laurie, a sixteen year old, asked a different question. Laurie told us at the opening of the session that she was born when her mother was fifteen.

Now, she and her mother lived with her grandmother. Laurie was upset because her grandmother told her and her mother what to do. Laurie said her mother wasn't independent anymore, and her mother wanted Laurie to stay home, not date until she was older, and not go away to college.

Laurie told us that, "My mother went into the woods when she had me, then she left the woods when I was born to go back home and live her mother's life. What can I do?"

I said, "You have your life to live. I think you're thinking about going into the woods. I think your mother makes her own choices. And remember, you may be surprised. No one, not even you knows what surprises there will be in your future."

How do you feel about my conversations with Laurie and Lin? What would you have said to them? I think about these conversations often. I also think that Sequoia's feelings for the woods are like the magic or fairies Sarah talked about. Both are probably our own true selves and best instincts looking after us.

Now you can understand why I've included so many girls' and women's stories in this book. Each of us has unique stories to tell.

The Green Stone

It's almost time to leave the past and talk about the present and the future. When we go into the future, girls take charge. We stage a talk show on the second Saturday of our program. In order for that to happen, the girls make plans by themselves at the end of the first session.

Everyone who's older than fifteen leaves the room. The girls have fifteen minutes to decide which topic(s) they'll use next week. I also ask the girls to evaluate the day we just spent and tell us what they liked and what they would change. Often, there's a big newsprint pad and markers left in the room for the girls to make their notes on.

While the girls are making plans inside the room, the older girls and women have a chance to talk outside the room. We also talk about our reactions to the day. Sometimes we decide what food to bring next week based on what we've heard the girls say they like. Pizza is the favorite lunch food, as long as we get veggie pizzas as well as meat pizzas, because there's always at least one girl (and me) who's a vegetarian.

Do you have a favorite food for lunch? Would you vote for pizza? For something else? Do you think it brings people closer together to eat together? Do your family and friends eat together?

We give the girls a five-minute warning. There's usually a lot of shocked voices as the girls realize more than half their time has vanished, but fifteen minutes seems to be a fair amount of time.

What would you be interested in hearing discussed in a talk show *for* girls run *by* girls? I usually display books for girls in the room, and the girls seem most interested in books about the changes their bodies experience. Most of the time, the talk show topics the girls choose have to do with their bodies.

What topics having to do with your body would you suggest for the talk show? Are there any other topics that interest you?

When the girls welcome us back into the room, one or two girls go over their evaluations. (Food is always on the list.) When they're finished, I ask the girls to think about how they'd organize a talk show. Next week, they'll share more ideas.

Now it's time to come together for our last story of the day — and our first picture book.

The story we're going to read is *Finding the Green Stone,* written by Alice Walker and illustrated with colorful paintings by Catherine Deeter. Right now, I'm looking at an original painting from the book. It's hanging on the wall next to me. The painting reminds me of girls who use pictures to express their emotions and ideas. There's definitely a story in each of Catherine's paintings and in the face of each of the people in them. If you go to a bookstore or a library, I know you will enjoy looking at them.

Alice is known to many girls because of the book, *The Color Purple,* which also was made into a movie. Alice says some of her stories, like *Finding the Green Stone,* come to her in her dreams. Reading Alice's book at this point in our day — it's nearly three o'clock, we're stretched out on the floor, some of us on our stomachs, some cross-legged, and some sitting up or leaning against a friend — catches us in a relaxed, almost dreamlike state. If you can get yourself comfortable, too, and feel relaxed, and hopefully, safe, then it's time to find out about green stones.

As I open the book, the last of our muffins is being eaten; but almost right away, food is forgotten and we seem to digest the story together, word by word. Remember when I mentioned earlier that we've recreated our past with the artifacts, and that we would move into the future? We're doing it now. One of the great things about moving into the future with Alice's story is that it tells us about a way to connect with the people around us.

I always read *Finding the Green Stone* in "Girls Speak Out," and each time listeners find some things that are different and some that are the same. I understand something new about the story whenever I read it. What stays the same during "Girls Speak Out" sessions is that everyone listens, almost without breathing, and everyone understands something about herself. But reading *Finding the Green Stone* when I'm alone is just as powerful as reading it aloud to other people. For me, no matter where I am or whom I'm with, it's what happens inside me that stays with me and inspires me. I wonder if you'll feel the same way.

Let's find out about green stones — together.

Right at this very time, in a small community on the Earth, live a brother and sister who have identical, iridescent green stones. The stones shine brightly and are small enough to fit into their hands. The children prize their stones and often play with them, taking them out of their pockets and holding them up to the sun, putting them in the clear water of the seaside among the rocks and plucking them out again, and so on. They are very happy with their stones.

But one day Johnny, the brother, lost his green stone. He looked everywhere for it.

Then he looked at his sister Katie's green stone, and, because his own stone was missing, he imagined that hers looked bigger and shinier than ever. He thought maybe his green stone had disappeared into hers.

"You've stolen my green stone!" he said.

"No way!" said Katie.

Johnny frowned at her and tried to grab her green stone — and even the memory of his own green stone vanished.

As the days passed, Johnny became very dull and sat for hours under the big tree in the center of the community.

But Katie never forgot that Johnny had once possessed his very own brightly glowing green stone, exactly like hers. And every day, while he sat under the tree fuming and casting mean looks at everybody who passed and sometimes muttering nasty things as well, she brought him her green stone to hold and reminded him that he had once had one, too.

At first, Johnny liked to play with Katie's stone, because whenever he did so he felt much better. But then he would remember that it was hers and that he did not have one of his own, and he would become angry.

One day, when Johnny was feeling this way, he tried to steal Katie's stone by pretending it was his.

"This is my green stone," he cried, clutching it in his fist, not intending to give it back, "not yours!"

But as soon as he did that, the stone turned gray in his hand, just like the rocks by the ocean, and when he looked over at Katie again she had her green stone, as bright and shining as ever!

Johnny felt sad. He realized that stealing somebody else's green stone would never make it his. Besides, it was lonely under the big tree, and trying to look mean all day was boring.

One day he mustered the courage to talk about his change of heart to Katie, who rarely talked to him now because she was afraid.

"I will never try to steal your green stone again," he said to her. "But I miss my own stone so much. Will you help me find it?"

At first Katie didn't know what to do. How could she believe Johnny meant what he said? That he would not try to grab her green stone?

"No," she said, after a long pause. "I can't help you at all."

At this point, we often pause in the reading to figure out what we might do. What would you say to Johnny?

Would you help him? Ten-year-old Alicia said she definitely *wouldn't* help *her* brother because he picks on her all the time. But each thing we do or don't do has a consequence.

Johnny's eyes were bright with unshed tears. Katie could see he meant her no harm, but something inside her liked being the powerful one for a change.

"No," she said again, sticking out her chest just as she'd seen Johnny do. But when she said "No" the second time, with a new coldness in her heart, her own green stone began to flicker and almost stopped shining!

Katie glanced at Johnny's sweet, sad face, so like her own, and then at her flickering green stone. Being spiteful to her brother would never work.

"I love you, Johnny," she said quietly. "I'm happiest when you have your very own green stone. I will do everything I can to help you find it."

The radiance of her stone, when she said this and reached for Johnny's hand, dazzled them both.

When Katie agreed to help, Alicia cried out, "No, she betrayed me." How do you feel about Katie's reaction? How do you feel about the different things that happened to Katie's stone as a result?

In their search for the green stone, Johnny and Katie ask for help from neighbors and their parents. Johnny's mother, who's busy as the town doctor, says:

"Listen, son, everybody has his or her green stone. You ought to know that by now. Nobody can give it to you and nobody can take it away. Only you can misplace or lose it. If you've lost it, it's your own fault. . . .

"We will get everybody in the community to help look for your green stone anyway."

But the search isn't successful. When everyone finally stops to rest under the big tree whose ". . . **green stone was one of its millions of fat green leaves,**" Johnny picks up a rock and he's feeling sad.

He was not crying just because he'd lost the green stone; he knew that because of his hurtful behavior, he deserved to lose it. He was crying because all these people, and especially Katie, loved him and were trying to help him find his green stone, even though they knew perfectly well he could only find it for himself! . . .

He was puzzled that everyone in his community wanted to help him do something he could only do himself, and in his puzzlement, he began to feel as if a giant bee were buzzing in his chest. It felt exactly as if all the warmth inside himself was trying to rush out to people around him. . . .

Katie explains to Johnny why everyone helped him search for something only he could find.

"We wanted to be with you when you found it!" said Katie, softly, wiping Johnny's tears away with her sleeve.

And sure enough, when Johnny followed Katie's gaze and looked down at his hand, what did he see? Not the dull and lifeless rock that he'd thought he was holding, but his very own bright green stone!

. . . . (All the people) welcomed the rising of a bright green sun in his heart, which they knew was Johnny's love for them, its warm light overflowing the small brown fingers clutched close to his chest.

Then the next one of Catherine Deeter's wonderful paintings shows everyone dancing around the tree, as if seen from the sky, and the tree is like a green stone. The next painting shows the whole continent, which also echoes the green stone. And the last painting shows the earth, like a green stone floating in the universe, because the unique and special place inside each of us is a small version of the universe outside.

"My true self just woke up from a loooonnnggg cat nap."
—Lydia

If we were in the same room right now, I would give you a green stone. It is exactly the same as the one I keep with me. I've also given green stones like this to hundreds of girls and women. You can draw, paint, or make yourself a green stone.

But even if you aren't holding a green stone, and even if you can't see one, you can imagine a beautiful green stone glowing inside you.

This is your true self. It is a place inside where you can go, and no one can follow you, no one can hurt you, and no one can change you. Everyone has this unique place. The green stone is only a symbol to remind us of this special place.

In this story Katie and Johnny each have a green stone that symbolizes their own world inside. It's important to remember that boys, too, have a unique self that can shine just like Johnny's green stone. How would you describe Katie's unique self? Johnny's unique self? What changes did each one go through to make their green stones shine? Why do you think each person in their community has a green stone — and why are they identical on the outside, even though each one belongs to only one person? And remember, the tree, the continents, and the earth are green stones, too. How does that make you feel?

You might want to draw or write about your feelings about being connected to other people and/or the planet. And if you want to think about experiences that make you feel isolated or disconnected, draw or write about them, too.

Twelve-year-old Kitty in Minneapolis told me that even though she could write about a lot of different feelings, her true self was mostly two of them, kind and funny. Miranda said her green stone was "feeling" itself; the power to feel. "Remember," she said, "girls have feelings."

Now's the time to begin thinking about who your true self is because you're going to be asked to write about yourself in a little while — and to read what other girls have written about their true selves.

During the week that follows the first session, I ask the girls to be their true selves, and to think what they can do to tap the power of that self.

When do you feel powerful? When do you feel most like yourself? If you write things down, you can look back and see if you have predicted your behavior. Maybe you'll surprise yourself with your ability to help yourself to be your best and truest self.

Right before we leave for the day, we have a ritual game, something we do at the end of both sessions. I call the game Tunnels and it's become a "rite of passage," which is an experience that marks a special event in our lives.

Tunnels is simple and fun to play: first, the women

stand in pairs, facing each other, with their hands stretched overhead forming a tunnel. (There can be a three-person hook-up if there's an extra woman.) Girls line up at one end of the tunnel made by the women, with plenty of clearance at the opposite end because they're going to run through the tunnel one at a time. They enjoy trying to be fast, and to make it to the end without being tickled.

It's the girls' turn now to let the women pass through their tunnel. If I'm lucky, I go first, before the girls have a chance to think of more and more ways to surprise the women as they run through. It's as if each group is giving the other permission to go on to future adventures; almost like giving birth to each other.

We're laughing and hugging as we leave.

Together Again

In South Carolina, on my way into the YWCA building for the second session of "Girls Speak Out," I heard someone excitedly calling my name. I turned around to see nine-year-old Anna come running to meet me in the doorway. When she caught my eye, she started waving her hand with the green stone in it and yelling, "My green stone was shining all week! My green stone was shining all week!" I remember this with tears in my eyes, the kind of tears that mean you're really happy.

At the first session, Anna had come with a group of girls who had been removed from their homes for their own safety from abusive or neglectful parents, and they were living together in a special group home. One of the counselors who traveled with them told me that Anna was depressed a lot and she might try to run away. When I told Anna what the counselor had said, I also told her I would like her to stay. Anna looked at me and said, "If I wanted to run away, I'd be gone by now because there are open doors all over this place."

During the morning, Anna was disappointed when the counselor told her that her picture couldn't be taken with the other girls because she was being hidden from her father who had sexually abused her. So Anna went on strike and didn't talk.

As the day went on, and pictures were being taken, Anna hid behind a small blackboard that was resting on the floor. She had drawn two arms, two legs, and a neck on it, and she would duck out of sight. She pretended it was her body that we could photograph.

While *Finding the Green Stone* was being read, she sat on a ledge next to me and drew. When I finished reading the story, she turned her pad around and showed us that it said "FEMALE" in very intricately decorated letters. She then took the video camera we were using and filmed everyone as she asked them if they were coming back next week. Her counselor told me she usually didn't appear interested in anything for more than a few minutes, and she was surprised Anna had stayed with us all day, and was talking and joking with us.

During the week, her mother sent Anna pictures of herself that she put on display. Anna's green stone had a special place on the table next to her bed, alongside a photograph of herself when she was a baby.

Sometimes when someone is angry, and as hurt and sad as Anna feels, I don't know what to do. Now I understand Anna has her own way of listening. I know, too, that her true self is also the girl flying across the parking lot, happy to be who she is and running into the room for another adventure in the second session.

The second session is different from the first session because there's less reading, and the girls do more talking. We know each other by now, just as you know more about "Girls Speak Out" from reading this book. The week between sessions seems to be a time when girls think a lot about what's on their minds that they want to talk about when they come back.

The girls and women who have been in the program tell me that they remember both sessions as exciting and happy times, but the talk in the second session can be more private and, as in the first session, it's confidential. It's often about things that are usually kept secret, about how people treat each other badly, even when they're in the same family or they're friends.

"Girls Speak Out" is a place where it's okay to talk about things that aren't usually mentioned in other places.

When we're together in the room at the beginning of the second session, it looks very different from the first Saturday. Think of the room as a rectangle, just like this page, and as the first session begins, the center space of the page is empty, but each corner holds four or five girls and women. In one city, the groups separated in the corners were different races and cultures: African-American girls in one corner, white girls in another, Latina girls and Vietnamese girls in the other two corners.

The connections made in the first session are visible in the second session. This time the center of the room is filled with girls. They're of different races, cultures, classes, and abilities. They're standing and laughing and talking together.

There's talk about where their green stones are, who lost theirs and who kept theirs, and who remembered to bring it today. Most of the girls have theirs with them, and some have brought the stones in holders they've made or improvised. Sometimes the stones are in a drawstring pouch on a ribbon around a girl's neck, the kind of pouch that holds a treasure you don't want to lose, and sometimes they're tied in fabric and hanging from a belt loop on a girl's jeans.

Playing a game at the start of the second session is another ritual I like to follow — we do the clapping game for as long as the girls want to, especially if there's anyone new in the room. There's also a new game to play called Who's in Charge?

We sit in a circle and begin Who's in Charge? by asking one girl to volunteer to leave the room and we ask her not to listen to what's going on inside while she's outside. When she's left, I explain that one girl in the room will be the leader, doing something like clapping her hands on her knees or tapping her shoulders. The rest of us have to imitate what she's doing, but we can't stare at her because the girl who's outside the room is coming in to guess who's in charge. We don't want to make it too easy.

Once our volunteer comes back in, she has three guesses. When she's done, whether she's guessed right or not, it's someone else's turn to be the leader. The leader from the previous round leaves the room, and a new leader is chosen by the girl who just guessed (or tried to guess) the leader.

Remember the clapping game from the first session? The same thing that happened there happens here: girls change the rules. For Who's in Charge?, we've had the "old" leader be the "new" leader. We've also decided no one's in charge, so we arranged for random switching of prearranged activities. Doing it randomly without a leader is really a lot of fun. It requires a different kind of concentration, and it gives the person who's outside the room something new to guess.

When we're finished with our opening game, we bring juice and food to the circle. The story we begin with comes from a novel named after its heroine, *Ellen Foster.* By this time in the program, girls know the routine and they do some of the storytelling. Sometimes a girl and I will take turns reading, or two girls may read together, especially if there's a conversation in the story.

Eleven-year-old Ellen is an unusual heroine. She's a very independent, white girl from a poor family in the South. Both parents neglect her and her father sexually abuses her. Ellen has grown up with bad feelings about her own class and other people's race, and these feelings confuse her. In particular, she struggles with her prejudices against a black girl, Starletta. One of the amazing things about Ellen is that she keeps her sense of humor, which means she also sees herself.

Ellen Foster is Kaye Gibbons' first book, and Kaye lives in the South, too, in North Carolina. Kaye wrote *Ellen Foster* in six weeks, and she says it was as if she was just talking out loud to the paper. At the beginning of the book, Ellen is pretty much alone in the world.

As the novel opens, Ellen begins with a surprising description of how she feels about her parents. One of the unusual things about Ellen is that she doesn't feel guilty about having angry feelings about her parents who treat her badly:

When I was little I would think of ways to kill my daddy. I would figure out this or that way and run it down through my head until it got easy.

The way I liked best was letting go a poisonous

spider in his bed. It would bite him and he'd be dead and swollen up and I would shudder to find him so. . . .

But I did not kill my daddy. He drank his own self to death the year after the county moved me out. I heard how they found him shut up dead in the house and everything. Next thing I know he's in the ground and the house is rented out to a family of four.

All I did was wish him dead real hard every now and then. And I can say for a fact that I am better off now than when he was alive. . . .

Oh but I do remember when I was scared. Everything was so wrong like somebody had knocked something loose and my family was shaking itself to death. Some wild ride broke and the one in charge strolled off and let us spin and shake and fly off the rail. And they both died tired of the wild spinning and wore out and sick. Now you tell me if that is not a fine style to die in. She sick and he drunk with the moving. They finally gave in to the motion and let the wind take them from here to there.

After Ellen's mother died, Ellen was left alone at home with her father. At her mother's funeral, Ellen says:

. . . . My daddy wonders if I plan to tell somebody the whole story. I do not know if there is a written down rule against what he did but if it is not a crime it must be a sin. It is one way or the other. And he wants to know if I'm telling.

> *"You have to love yourself before you can love anyone else."*
>
> —*Keosha*

One day at school, Ellen's teacher notices a bruise on Ellen's arm. Ellen calls her father's sexual abuse of her "the squeeze." Her teacher arranges for Ellen to live with another family. Ellen goes from family to family until she sees a woman who has lots of foster kids. Ellen decides she wants to live with them — and she does. She moves in with the family in the brick house where the school bus stops.

As *Ellen Foster* ends, there is still one person in Ellen's life Ellen wants to tell something important to — it's her friend, Starletta. Ellen invites Starletta to spend the night in her new house.

Starletta I've looked forward to you coming to my house and I hope you have a fine time here. I sure like it here. Do you remember me living with my daddy and how I used to come to your house so much?

I sure do she says to me and it takes twice as long for her to get that out as normal because she stutters bad and she gets frustrated.

Well I came to your house so much because I did not want to be with my daddy and mostly because I like you so much. Even if my daddy was the president

I would have still run down to your house whenever I needed to play. Do you believe me?

And I look at her so she can nod and will not need to speak.

She hates to talk.

Starletta I always thought I was special because I was white and when I thought about you being colored I said to myself it sure is a shame Starletta's colored. I sure would hate to be that way . . . the three of you live in that house that's about to fall down. I always went away from your house wondering how you stood to live without an inside toilet. I know your daddy just put one in but you went a long time without one. Longer than any white folks I know. And when I thought about you I always felt glad for myself. And I don't know why. I really don't. And I just wanted to tell you that. You don't have to say anything back. You just lay there and wait for supper.

And I will lay here too and wait for supper beside a girl that every rule in the book says I should not have in my house much less laid still and sleeping by me.

But while I watch her sleep now I remember they changed that rule. So it does not make any sense for me to feel like I'm breaking the law.

Nobody but a handful of folks I know pays attention to rules about how you treat somebody anyway. . . .

I came a long way to get here but when you think

about it real hard you will see that old Starletta came even farther. . . .

And all this time I thought I had the hardest row to hoe.

That will always amaze me.

The room is usually very quiet for a while after this reading. Anita, a nine-year-old girl in northern California, had a unique reaction. She burst out and said, "Girls have something men want. Men aren't going to get it. Men and boys have nothing exciting happening to them so they try to take it from us."

Anita, Ellen, and Anna were all talking about things which usually aren't talked about by or with young girls, things like neglect, poverty, sexual abuse, physical abuse, verbal abuse, incest, and racial bias in ourselves. Girls struggle when things like this happen to them. Being alone makes it harder. And having no information is a part of that loneliness. What happened to Ellen, she learns, is against the law, and it happens to some little boys, too. Ellen found people who helped her get out of a bad situation.

Telling, like Ellen did, can be very hard, but it's often the only way other people can know what's happening to children, especially when it's family members or friends who betray a child's trust in them. Girls tell me that telling someone they trust, who believes them, makes a big difference in their lives.

Has anyone ever told you a secret? Have you ever wanted to tell your own secret? Trusting yourself to know when and who to tell secrets to is an important part of being true to yourself.

Five years ago, when she was fourteen, my niece spent the night at her best friend's house. She fell asleep on the living room floor and the other girls were in the bedroom. Yulahlia woke up during the night, and her friend's father was undressing her. He raped her.

His six-year-old daughter was asleep on the couch so my niece didn't make any noise because she didn't want her to wake up and be frightened by what her father was doing. Yulahlia didn't tell anyone. She went home in the morning and took a shower.

A month later, she told her boyfriend, and he told her father. When I found out, I took her to a doctor to make sure she was tested for AIDS and other diseases. She was physically healthy. My niece is part Puerto Rican and we live in a mostly white community. After talking to lawyers and judges, we decided that it would be almost impossible to get a fair trial, both because of prejudice, and because my niece hadn't told right away while there was still evidence of rape.

I found a woman therapist who works with young girls who are survivors of rape. My niece was in counseling until last year, when she went away to college. She's the only one of her friends to go to college, and she's proud she got a scholarship and did all the applying herself.

When we were unpacking her clothes and stuffed animals in her dorm room right before school began, my niece told me she wanted to change her name. She explained, "I'm a new person here. I'm a happy person here." She changed her first name, and she's become a writer.

She told me recently, "I never thought I would say this, but the rape made me rethink who I am. I was into partying and drinking then. And he made me feel like nothing. Now I think, why should some man make *me* feel that way. I'm a great person, really. And now I know it."

Even if something very bad happens to you, you can use it to become who you want to be. You can take control of your life, just like my niece did.

How do Ellen's and Yulahlia's stories make *you* feel? People who study young girls say that one of the characteristics of nine- and ten-year-old girls is that they say what they feel out loud, especially when something's unfair. Girls' voices remind me how wonderful it feels to say, from the inside out, in our own way, "It's not fair!"

Have you had any experiences you want to tell someone? Good ones and/or bad ones? Writing or drawing is a way of telling what's happening to you, too, if words are hard, but you'll know when you're ready, just as other girls have.

You may want to write about your ideas on how to be a good friend and protector, especially of yourself. Linda, a twelve-year-old girl in San Diego, told us she had a friend who was an incest victim — which means that someone in her own family was abusing her. Her friend kept it a secret until she told Linda. Now Linda is encouraging her to tell a grown-up she trusts. In the meantime, Linda says, she's careful to protect her friend's privacy and safety, and her own feelings.

Of course, some girls have much different experiences from Anita, Ellen, and Anna. Two sisters who came to "Girls Speak Out" in New York City spoke freely in both sessions about subjects that are usually taboo. Their parents wanted to meet me because I wanted the girls to come back to more sessions and give me advice, so we arranged a visit to their apartment in Harlem.

Susan and Allan, the girls' parents, grew up in the same two-block area where they now live with their daughters, ten-year-old Tina and thirteen-year-old

Stephanie. I visited on a Saturday in July when Allan and Susan were home from work, and Susan's sister stopped by with her two-year-old grandson.

Tina was at the kitchen table with us, painting with watercolors, decorating a picture of a hot air balloon, and she listened attentively as her mother talked about "telling children the truth." Susan said she told both girls about problems like sexual abuse when they were ten years old. Tina said she felt better knowing what could happen, and she said her mother told her if someone bothered her, even if it was her or her father, another relative or friend, Tina should tell someone.

"It makes me feel safe," Tina told me. "I like knowing what to do."

Allan brought us cold drinks, then he sat down and leaned forward in his seat, with his chin in his hands.

"I'm proud of my daughters," he said. "We wish they could travel and see more of this country, and maybe they will do more than we have. I hope so."

Stephanie was preparing her high school applications, and when she came into the kitchen, we talked about her choices.

"Something good will happen, sooner or later. That's what I believe, you know," Stephanie told me as I left.

"Don't let Harlem's reputation keep you from walking downtown on a nice day like this. You'll be okay," Allan reminded me.

As I walked to my friend Gloria's house, I was thinking about how hopeful this family is about life. I couldn't wait to tell her how good it was to be with a family that talks openly about their feelings across the kitchen table — and to someday share this experience with you, too.

Now that the first storytelling is over, we're ready to go around the circle to discuss the week between sessions. Sometimes we take a break. After we stretch and settle back down, I ask the girls and women to also talk about whether they had a chance to be powerful and their true selves.

As one fourteen-year-old girl said, "We've had times last week that were sacred and afterwards you feel so close."

In South Carolina, one of the women, thirty-three-year-old Roberta, was the first to speak. She told us that two important things had happened to her during the week, and they both involved the green stone. First, she had held her green stone in her hand when she asked for a raise at work: She manages a store and when she was promoted to manager, she didn't get a raise. She got one this time because she said, "I felt like it was fair and asking was what I needed to do." The green stone had given her the courage to ask for what she thought she deserved.

Roberta then told us she was going to divorce her husband. She said "he can't be a good father" to her two daughters, ages two and twelve. She said the green stone is a reminder to her that she could have a "better life."

One of the last to talk that morning was Jasmine, a twelve-year-old girl. She started by telling us her week started out awful. Her brother, who's seventeen, is a drug addict. He's been living away from home, but Jasmine told us he came back and stole "everything that's precious to us." He even took her collection of glass animals. Jasmine said he's in jail now and that she felt sad about that.

Roberta spoke again: "Jasmine, I'm sorry about your brother. I want you to know you're braver than I was. When I talked about my husband, about how I was leaving him, I didn't tell the whole truth, the real reason I'm leaving. My husband is a drug addict, just like your brother. When you were talking about your brother, I realized I had been ashamed to talk about my husband. I thought it was my job to make him stop using drugs. He's making our lives miserable.

"But I think I can do something to help my daughters — and myself. I want to thank you. I want you to know you're not alone. There's a lot of us."

Jasmine also told us that even though she was sad about her brother, she was angry at him, too. Having these different feelings at once, she said, was "okay, not a problem." Jasmine had also written in her journal for the first time during the week; maybe, she said, she'd write a story about her brother. Writing things down privately does help us to understand them.

In other cities, girls said different things. Jen, who's ten and lives in northern California, told us she "felt physically and emotionally stronger all week." In New York City, six girls all between the ages of fifteen and eighteen discovered they "didn't have time" to be their true selves. They were involved in so many activities, including long phone conversations helping other girls and boys with problems, that they felt they had no time to concentrate on themselves. Sharon, a seventeen year old, said "she feels pressure to take advantage of every opportunity to add another activity to my college application."

One sixteen-year-old girl took me aside and said, "This may sound weird, Andrea, but my green stone made me feel better all week." I told her I thought she was feeling good about herself, and she agreed, "That's it. That's what it is."

One ten year old in West Virginia brought more than her green stone to the second session. Meghan brought a small wooden box full of what she described as "all the things that are most important to me in the world." She opened the lid and inside the box was a collection of objects, each with a story.

"Here's my favorite book, *A Wrinkle in Time,* that's about finding good no matter where you travel in the universe. This is a kachina doll I made in school in third grade, and this is a dream catcher I bought at a street fair last year."

Meghan took out a blue plastic calculator that was missing the display screen. Although the calculator was broken, it was clean and new looking.

"I don't know why I keep this," Meghan said. "I found it in the park, took it home, cleaned it up, and put it in my box. I've had it for about a year now."

The girl sitting next to Meghan said, "Maybe you keep it to remind you that you have power inside you, not in a machine and you don't need a machine to be powerful."

Meghan said she was worried she wasn't being her true self. But that morning, she got up early with her dad and they listened to music together.

"My dad loves music," she said, "and so do I. When we were listening to Bach together, well, I love it so much, it felt so good, I knew it then.

"My true self is music. Music makes me feel all kinds of things. About love, and how my dad loves baseball, especially one player, Keith Hernandez. Keith Hernandez plays baseball because he loves it. Most of the other players do it for money. I've been thinking a lot about money.

"I think greed is the reason for a lot of problems. I think it happens all over the world. And not just to people; we get greedy about nature and animals, too. When we forget about our true selves, we get greedy."

Fourteen-year-old Yvonne, who goes to a middle school in Harlem returned to the second session with a story about school. She asked right away if she could read to us, and she seemed excited. Her friends from school who were there were teasing her because she was reading out loud, but she ignored them and went right on reading. Then she told her story about being her true self.

During the week, in Yvonne's English class, they had been discussing a book, *That Was Then, This Is Now.* Yvonne said that the boys in the class were making it impossible to talk. The book is about two boys who are friends, and Yvonne's male classmates were calling the characters "homos" and "fags." They were disrupting what anyone else said, especially Yvonne, because she openly disagreed with them.

The teacher asked the boys to be quiet. Yvonne told them to be quiet. She said she wanted to talk about the book without their noise. They didn't stop. Yvonne got up from her seat, said she'd be right back, and left the classroom.

"I marched down the hall, around the corner and into the principal's office. I told her that it was her job to make sure I could learn. I said the boys were making it impossible for me to learn anything. They were making rude remarks about the book, and I didn't appreciate them or their sexist remarks."

While she was telling us what she did, Yvonne kept on looking down and tying and retying her shoelaces. The girls from her school who teased her earlier, when she was reading, were now quiet. She continued.

"Well, the principal got up and told me to come with her back to my class. She went into the room with me, and the boys were still laughing. The principal told the boys that they would have detention and everyone would stay in at lunch to talk about what happened during class.

"What I don't understand," Yvonne said, "is that later on in the day, some of the boys thanked me."

I thought when I heard Yvonne say this about the boys in her class that they're like Johnny in *Finding the Green Stone*, even though she didn't think of it that way, and she was like Katie. The boys were grateful because Yvonne was giving them the chance to be free of the pressure to be thoughtless. They really wanted to be friends with girls, but they found it hard to do that in their school.

Yvonne's friend, Maria, interrupted to say, "Some of the boys told us they didn't like what the others were saying, but they thought it was better to go along with the program."

Yvonne said, "Well, I'm glad it was me who got up and complained. I know I'm going to make it, that being a girl is tough in class, but I'm getting good grades and I know where I'm going. I've made up my mind."

Her friends were now encouraging Yvonne to continue her story.

"The principal said that she was going to change the punishment system. She said students should be rewarded when they do good things, and not just punished for getting into trouble. She called my mom and my mom called my aunts and now my whole family knows. Now everyone's talking about what I did, like it was some big deal." Yvonne was smiling down at her boots as she finished talking.

In California, during the first session, a sixth-grader had talked about drugs on her campus. Doreen said some of her friends were smoking pot during recess and offering her some. "I feel afraid when they offer it to me," she said. "And I don't know what to do."

Doreen decided to tell the principal. She talked it

over with her mother, and decided she wanted to do it alone. Her mother said she should tell the principal to call home if he wanted to talk to her, too. Doreen said she was nervous. One of her friends who kept offering her drugs didn't have a supportive family, and Doreen said smoking pot made her friend feel accepted at school. It's a small school in a rural area, and Doreen was worried about what could happen to the kids.

"The principal really didn't do anything," Doreen told us with a shrug of her shoulder. "He said it was hard to catch kids in the act, and he didn't want to do anything illegal. I think I knew nothing much was going to happen, but I had to do it anyway. My mom says she's going to get on the school board. If there was someone else who felt the same way I do, I think I'd do a petition or something. It just makes me feel better, I guess."

What memorable experiences have you had at school? Can you make a list of what you'd like to change? How do you feel about what Yvonne and Doreen did? Do you have any other suggestions about how they might have acted? You may want to describe what school means to you.

Esmeralda Santiago writes about being a young girl and teenager in *When I Was Puerto Rican*. She moved from a small town in Puerto Rico to New York City.

Her first lessons about school in Puerto Rico are like those in most countries, they're filled with *supposed-tos:*

I started school in the middle of the hurricane season, and the world grew suddenly bigger, a vast place of other adults and children whose lives were similar, but whose shadings I couldn't really explore out of respect and *dignidad. Dignidad* was something you conferred on other people, and they, in turn, gave it back to you. It meant you never swore at people, never showed anger in front of strangers, never stared, never stood too close to people you'd just met. . . . It meant adults had to be referred to as Don so-and-so, and Dona so-and-so, except for teachers who you should call Mister or Missis so-and-so. It meant if you were a child, you did not speak until spoken to, did not look an adult in the eye, did not raise your voice nor enter or leave a room without permission. It meant adults were always right, especially if they were old. It meant men could look at women any way they liked but women could never look at men directly, only in sidelong glances. . . . It meant you didn't gossip, tattle, or tease. It meant men could say things to women as they walked down the street, but women couldn't say anything to men, not even to tell them to go jump in the harbor and leave them alone.

All these rules entered our household the minute I

was allowed to leave for the long walk to and from school. It wasn't that I hadn't learned them before. . . .

But these rules had little to do with the way we lived at home. In our family we fought with vigor, adults as well as children, even though we knew we weren't supposed to. We yelled across the room at one another, came in and out of our one-room house without saying "excuse me" and "may I come in," or even knocking. . . . We children spoke whenever we felt like it, interrupted our parents all the time, and argued with them until Mami finally reminded us that we had stepped over the line of what was considered respectful behavior towards parents.

Lily is a nineteen-year-old Puerto Rican woman going to college in San Jose, California. She said that when she was growing up, she had been told not to touch valuable things that didn't belong to her. In the first session, she noticed that Latina girls were reluctant to pick up and handle the artifacts. Lily explained to the girls that the rules were different in "Girls Speak Out."

Differences in ideas on how to behave can be *cultural*; that is, rules we learn from parents, relatives, and seeing what people around us do. I think of cultural differences as behavior and ideas we learn from *the outside in,* but it's important to understand them so you don't misinterpret what other people do. (For instance, in some

African traditions, it's a sign of respect for young people to look down at the floor when talking to elders, but in this country people equate honesty with "looking you in the eye.")

Even people in the same culture may share none, some, or all of the same rules. In "Girls Speak Out," knowing about cultural differences has brought us closer together: it would've been easy to think the Latina girls didn't like the artifacts, but once Lily spoke up, we all had a great time holding and passing them around. It felt like a party.

There are some cultural practices that do permanent physical damage to females. A woman who came here from Africa didn't want her young daughters to be victims of *female genital mutilation* (FGM). In much of Africa, proponents of FGM surgically remove part or all of a young girl's outer genitals, especially the clitoris, so she won't be able to feel sexual pleasure and be tempted to "misbehave." Girls' vaginas are often sewn closed so they can't have intercourse until they're married. It's a very painful practice, and also a damage to health.

The African girls' mother stayed in the United States in order to protect her daughters from FGM in their native country. The girls didn't come to "Girls Speak Out" because they still didn't feel safe.

Mimi, an Ethiopian woman who's living in California, explained that female genital mutilation is practiced by some Africans living in the United States. Mimi had been a victim of FGM in her own country when she was six years old, and she had recently asked her mother why she let it happen to her. Her mother told Mimi she was following tradition, that she and her mother, Mimi's grandmother, were also victims. Her mother said she was sorry it happened to Mimi. She traveled with Mimi to villages in Ethiopia and urged women not to allow their daughters to be mutilated. This is not easy because a girl may not be considered marriageable without it.

I've learned more about other cultures as I traveled doing "Girls Speak Out." Mary, a young woman in Oregon, had a Japanese-American boyfriend, and she brought his two teenage sisters to the first session. During the week between sessions, they told her they were uncomfortable because girls and women in "Girls Speak Out" had talked about sex, sexual abuse, and neglect. The Japanese-American girls had been taught not to talk in public about "personal matters." Because they had also been taught not to bring attention to themselves, they didn't talk to us about their feelings during the session.

When Mary told me the sisters didn't want to come

back to the second session, we worked out an arrange-ment: Mary would leave with them if they were un-comfortable.

A woman writer who helped me develop "Girls Speak Out" is Chinese-American. Martha was at a ses-sion with girls who were in counseling for sexual abuse. Months after the session, Martha told me she felt "frozen" with the girls. She had never been around girls who talked so openly about such difficult experiences, and it was hard for her to feel okay about them. She wasn't neglected or abused during her childhood. She felt it was awful for girls to be treated so badly, and she was trying to overcome the cultural behavior she learned as a girl. Martha wants to be more open to peo-ple with different kinds of experiences.

To go back to the book, *When I Was Puerto Rican,* one of the rules in Esmeralda's culture is that women stay at home, but Esmeralda's mother works outside the house in a factory:

I got the message that my mother was breaking a taboo that I'd never heard about. The women in the neighborhood turned their backs on her when they saw her coming, or, when they talked to her, they scanned the horizon, as if looking at her would infect them with whatever had made her go out and get a job.

"Always speak your mind and that's when you're powerful."
—Shakoiya

Esmeralda isn't happy either when her mother tells her what she's doing:

"Where are you going?"

"There's a new factory opening in Toa Baja. Maybe they need people who can sew."

"Who's going to take care of us?"

"Gloria will be here in a little while. You can help her with the kids. I've already made dinner."

"Will you work every day?"

"If they hire me."

"So you won't be around all the time."

"We need the money. . . ."

Mami twisted and sprayed her hair, powdered her face, patted rouge on already pink cheeks, and spread lipstick over already red lips. . . . I wanted to find a rag and wipe that stuff off her face, the way she wiped off the dirt and grime that collected on mine. She turned to me with a large red smile.

"What do you think?"

I was ashamed to look, afraid to speak what I saw.

"Well?"

. . . . I couldn't help the tears that broke my face into a million bits, which made her kneel and hold me. I wrapped my arms around her, but what I felt was not Mami but the harsh bones of her undergarments. I buried my face in the soft space between her neck and shoulder, and sought there the fragrance of oregano and rosemary, but all I could come up with was Cashmere Bouquet and the faint flowery dust of Maybelline.

At the end of the book, Esmeralda is about to begin high school. She and her mother are living in New York City. One day she tells her mother

"I hate my life!" I yelled.
"Then do something about it," she yelled back.

Esmeralda follows her mother's advice and example. She auditions for a special high school in New York City that encourages students to act, write, and be artists and musicians. Her life changes when she discovers that being creative, especially as a writer, makes her happy.

As I mentioned before, there is a lot more talking by girls in the second session. The stories you've just read are examples of what is said as we go around the circle at the beginning of the session. When we've finished going around the circle, and we've had a break, I change the routine. Instead of calling the girls together with a story, I give them back their own stories. If they've requested it, they've been printed and bound in our "Girls Speak Out" books.

In the first session, we talked about the fact that female human beings are missing from history books. Now we have our own book of girls and women's history. It's exciting to have a history book about us, especially one that we've written ourselves. Stories the girls wrote about their artifacts are in our book. There's a membership list to enable the girls to stay in touch. There's also a list of good books that have been published for girls. You'll find a list at the back of this book, too.

You can make your own book just as we do in "Girls Speak Out." Then you can show it to other people. Your journal or notebook may be private and not for other people's eyes, but if you're like me, there are probably some writings and/or drawings you'd like to share with other people. Some girls hand out copies to their friends. Some girls have shown their creations to a lot of people.

Being creative on paper or in any other way that satisfies you can be either private or public. It's another choice you may make for yourself.

Doing a Talk Show

Now it's time for girls to create their own talk show. Our talk shows are "live" and unrehearsed. However, you may want to write a script for a talk show you can try out with some friends. Or you may want to follow the live format.

Girls created the talk show idea at the very beginning of "Girls Speak Out" sessions. It's been the chosen activity in every second session except one. In that session, girls talked for hours without using the talk show format. They asked each other and the women question after question. We stayed an extra hour until finally we had to leave the room.

As I mentioned earlier, girls and their bodies is the most popular talk show topic. In our "Girls Speak Out" sessions, we haven't discussed more than one topic because time flies. Other topics that have been voted on include "Children Having Children," "The Way People Portray Females in Today's World," and "Should Teachers Put their Hands on Other People's Children?"

The girls decide who's going to be the person who

asks the questions, who's the announcer, and who will be the guests and "experts." We've had girls handle props and act as producers and backstage help, too. The women are in the audience asking questions and sharing experiences in response to the girls' questions.

In order to get ready, everyone over fifteen usually leaves the room because, after all, this is "Girls Speak Out." It's their day. Twenty minutes is the average time the girls spend choosing roles and questions and setting up the "studio."

Chairs are arranged for the audience in rows or in a semicircle. Four or five chairs face the audience.

You may draw a floor plan in your notebook for a talk show that's designed especially for girls, and think of a title you like.

The girls wrap a marker in construction paper, transforming it into a microphone. During the show, it's passed back and forth from speaker to speaker. There's a sign on an easel with the name of the talk show and the topic. Sometimes the talk show is named for a girl, usually the hostess, or the city or town we're in. There are breaks for commercials, but what usually happens is the girls are so busy organizing the show itself that there's no time to prepare commercials. We've stayed commercial-free.

When the women and older girls are called back into the room, we find seats. The girls who are onstage try to stay out of sight until the audience is seated and the announcer comes out.

I'm always delighted that we spontaneously applaud each other, and don't need encouragement.

Our talk show guests are usually in categories like "friends" who have different opinions about how to dress, when to date, and whether to have sex. Sometimes there are "mothers" and "daughters."

The "experts" usually forget about the book they're holding as a prop. Instead, they talk about their own experiences and feelings. "Experts" have said the following:

"I have a diagnosis. It's a state of being mixed-up."

Another said, "We're on TV and we want to pretend we recycle our water cups."

When a hostess asked an expert to give her opinion to a mother and daughter who disagreed about what age the daughter could date, the expert shook her head no.

She said, "They're already up to the limit of being influenced."

Disagreements have been strong about whether a girl can do what she wants and not care what other people think of her, especially when it comes to how she dresses. Two girls in Minneapolis argued about whether a girl has a responsibility to her friend as well as to herself.

"My true self is being generous."
—Melissa

"I don't want to be with you when you wear sexy stuff," one girl said to her talk show friend. "You look like you want boys all over you."

Her friend said it was her business how she dressed, and she didn't care what boys thought.

"You look like you're asking for it," her friend argued.

"I'm not, and I can dress anyway I want to."

The talk show "personality" said, "I think we can go outside in a flannel nightgown, wearing a bag over our heads, and guys would still give us trouble."

Have you any feelings about what you or other girls wear? Can you make any suggestions about clothing for girls? How safe do you feel when you leave your house? Are some places safer than others? What would you wear if you could wear anything you wanted to?

In San Diego, the audience and the panel began a conversation. They exchanged experiences about whether it was ever "too late" or "Could you be too old?" to do something, like go to school and start a new career. The girls led the discussion from the stage and someone ran through the audience with the microphone, which started to disintegrate from so much handling.

One woman, Cindy, said she had been to a woman's conference in China, and she discovered that Chinese orphans had very hard lives. She decided to adopt a

Chinese baby girl. She and her husband are fifty-four and their other children are grown-up. Cindy said, "You're never too old."

Nine-year-old Becky said she loved playing soccer at school, but the boys always complained about having a girl on their team. She was also tired of being the last person picked to play, and of the faces the boys made when her name was finally called. Becky's friends told her she'd never change the boys' attitude.

When they had to choose players this week, Becky said she told the boys how she felt about their attitude. She stood in the middle of the group, and asked them how they would feel if they were treated like they had no feelings. "I know you care about winning, and I can help you win," she told them, "but you have to be fair." She said she felt better. The boys listened, and Becky said she'd do it again and again "if I have to."

Ruth's just started school, and she's studying to become a teacher. Ruth married just after she graduated from high school, and her husband died recently. She's forty-four, and said she "never imagined" she'd be able to support herself and her family.

I talked about graduating from law school when I was forty. I had always wanted to be a lawyer, but when I was young, I was told that girls didn't grow up to be lawyers. Well, it turned out that I didn't either, but I still wanted to learn about law and how the legal system works. Law school gave me confidence to try new things, like becoming an investigative reporter and building a house on a mountaintop.

Girls in New York City wanted to talk about sexual harassment in their school. Although they didn't like it, the girls said that sexual harassment was part of what happens when a girl's body changes. *Sexual harassment* means words or actions, especially, but not only by teachers or someone who has power over you, that focus on your body, make you feel uncomfortable, and keep you from working well in school or on the job.

The girls had a problem with a principal at their school who was "always putting his hands on our backs, heads, and our shoulders. He's always rubbing us and laughing about it." In South Carolina, a teacher and other students referred to how the girls' bodies looked in ways that made them feel uncomfortable.

The teacher said things like, "You're too pretty to worry about that" and "You look good in short skirts."

"It's like you're a thing, not a person," said Loretta. Boys in gym class teased the girls about bras and developing breasts. Running and playing sports that made a girl's breasts bounce brought on a lot of the boys' comments and made the girls not want to run. Most of the adults to whom the girls complained didn't think it was so bad. They said things like, "Boys will be boys" and "What did you expect now that you're becoming a woman?"

When I was teaching in a middle school, and my students were in sixth to eighth grade, I was also writing for a newspaper in northern California. I worked with and wrote about four girls I knew who had been sexually harassed by their high school drama teacher. My son Jesse had gone to the same high school as the girls. When I started working with them, I asked him if he knew what was happening between the girls and their teacher. He told me everyone knew something was going on, but no one ever really talked about it. When one of the girls said Jesse could read her description of what happened, I remember the look on his face as he handed it back to me. I think it changed him because he said, "I had no idea what it felt like to be her in that situation. I wish it hadn't happened, and that I understood what it felt like. I was senior class president, and maybe I could have done something to help." When I told her what Jesse had said, she didn't feel so alone.

The girls and I discovered that teachers, principals, and other people working in schools don't know it's against the law for girls to be sexually harassed by adults or other students. They think that sexual harassment laws are only for grown-ups in the workplace. A lot of the people outside the school system needed to learn about girls' rights, too. As girls and people in the community worked together, we became "experts."

Sometimes the girls ask me to be a guest on their talk show, and tell what happened to the girls in California. It surprises me how many girls across the country, in big cities and small towns, have had similar experiences to the girls I've worked with.

The law that protects children in school is called Title IX. Title IX says that girls and boys are guaranteed an equal education, free from harassment and discrimination. Harassing or restricting you based on your gender, race, sexual preference, ability, or religion is illegal. Each school is supposed to let students and their families know about their rights under Title IX. Knowing about the law helped the girls I was working with, but it still took a long time for the teacher to lose his California teaching credential, and then he went to another state to teach.

One of the girls I worked with in California is named Willow. Willow realized she could do something about being sexually harassed in 1992, when she heard Anita Hill on television. Anita Hill was a witness against Clarence Thomas, who wanted a lifetime job as a judge on the United States Supreme Court. Anita said Clarence Thomas had sexually harassed her years before when he was her boss.

Willow says she learned from Anita Hill's testimony

that it was against the law for someone in authority to treat people unfairly because of their sex, and she complained to her school about her teacher. Some girls in "Girls Speak Out" are worried that they could "get into trouble for telling on a teacher." They wonder if you "get a bad grade?"

Willow says telling was "scary. I stopped going to drama practice after school, and then I dropped the drama class." But, she says, "it was worse when he was harassing me and other girls. I hated having him touching me and talking to me about his wife and having sex.

"I'm glad I complained. A lot of other girls told me they had the same problem with him. Some of the other girls were angry because they thought he was a good teacher, but I didn't want him to do it to other girls. It took a long time to make him stop, but it was worth it. I couldn't have done it alone. I'm glad there were other girls and women in our community, and I had my mother to help out.

"If I could say something to girls, I'd tell them to believe in themselves. I think most of us know when something is wrong, but we don't listen to our instincts."

Anita Hill says it was hard for her to talk about what happened to her, especially on television. She took her mother and father with her to Washington, DC, when she went to talk about Clarence Thomas to the committee in the U.S. Senate that was deciding whether he could be a Supreme Court justice.

One of Anita's sisters is a fourth-grade teacher in Oklahoma. She went into her principal's office to see Anita on television when Anita was testifying. The men from the Senate who were questioning Anita obviously didn't believe her. Her sister could see how hard it was for Anita, so she arranged to leave school that day, and she went to Washington, DC, to support Anita. When she returned, her class was glad she had gone even though they missed her. Anita's whole family came to support her when she spoke out.

Anita says, "Now that I've found my voice, I'm never going to be silent." Do you think you would feel the same way as Anita and Willow? What suggestions do you have about stopping sexual harassment?

"Pretending" to be an expert can lead to actually becoming an expert. That's just one of the many examples of what you can learn from putting together your own talk show, and talking about what's happening to you and your friends.

I hope reading about these talk shows helps you explore some of the possibilities open to you.

Being a Daughter

By now, we're almost at the end of the second session. We put the room back together after the talk show so we can sit on the floor. Sitting in a circle brings us together again, girls and women, side by side.

The reading I do now is unusual because it's a mixture of selections. We'll be reading parts of three different books about girls who are trying to understand what it means to them to become women.

In *Little Jordan*, Marly Youmans' first novel, thirteen-year-old Meg has a special summer where

> my weeks at the beach blended into one week, one day . . . I learned about distance and about seeing at close range that summer. I believed what I touched with my hands. That summer I was busy running up against things, learning what they meant.

Meg also begins to look at boys differently, and they see her differently, especially Fred Massey, who

"The things that I think make me a young woman are my heart, mind, and body."

—Andy

was fifteen, (and) good looking, . . . He had the sort of intent expression on his face that makes people say that somebody's eyebrows are drawn together. Honestly, my stomach dropped an inch or two when I met his blue eyes. Not that I stood alone in that kind of behavior. Half the girls in our school had crushes on Fred Massey.

Meg and Fred share time and secrets over the next weeks.

"You're a strange girl, Meg," Fred said. He sighed, as if he'd been holding his breath.

Neither of us said a word for a long time.

"I guess I'll go home some day soon," he said, sitting up.

"Because I'm strange?" I felt sure I would cry, partly because Fred was going home . . . .

"No." Fred laughed then, and he put his arm around my shoulders — touching me for the first time. He gazed up at the hill fields . . . .

"Yesterday," he said, still looking up at the hills, "my mom told me that running away from one thing just leads you to chase after another."

That gave me a quirk of surprise, and I was busy puzzling over what it meant when Fred leaned closer and rubbed his face against mine. Then he kissed me . . . very quietly. Quiet as dew. For a minute I saw his eyelashes against his skin and felt his cheek, cool and smooth like a little boy's cheek.

Maybe all first kisses are the same, or maybe none of them are. Mine started with thinking about a boy's mother, a boy's cheek. Then suddenly everything seemed to change, as though I had stepped into deep water, and I closed my eyes.

Have you imagined what your first romantic kiss would be like? Have you experienced it already? Meg says her first kiss changes her. How do you feel about a romantic relationship? Could it be that powerful? Which relationships are most important to you?

Meg's feelings for her grandmother are important to her, especially as she discovers more about who she is.

My grandma met me on the bleached, silvery porch, and I loved her more than ever, even though earlier I had thought maybe I was getting so grown-up that a grandmother might not mean as much. Because in between visits you forget how she smells of lilacs and how soft her skin is, you forget how an old person is really just as interesting as anybody else, maybe more so if we're talking about my grandparents.

Meg spends an afternoon with her grandmother on the water, exploring tidal creeks in her grandmother's canoe. Meg is asking her grandmother about her hair, which is

coiled in a neat wheel at the nape of her neck.

"When you let down your hair —" I hesitated.

Grandma thrust the canoe off a snag.

"How long is it?" I asked.

"Why did you think of that? I don't know. Long. Not so long as it used to be. Old people droop and change. Noses get bigger, ears and feet, too. Hair, hair thins and breaks."

"You must have had an awful lot of hair when you were young," I said.

"Yes, I did. Everyone said thick hair was a woman's great beauty, but I hardly knew what to do with it all."

Grandma stared down at the curved banks . . . .

I had a sudden vivid picture of Grandma like Eve in an oil painting, a young and pretty Eve with scads of silvery hair. Only of course it wouldn't be silver. It would be a color like mine. It would sweep over her bare shoulders, splashing past her feet. My grandpa, with his young man's hands, would be weaving his fingers through her hair, unplaiting and combing out her braids.

Somewhere beyond the frame where they played as lovers and Grandpa combed my grandma's hair,

Momma would be snoozing, a baby, her mouth open like a bird's. I lay there too, half of me, an infinitely small egg sleeping in my child-Momma's body.

Now here was my grandma, talking to me as though I was a grown woman.

"At night he combed my hair until it untangled and the brush sank through easily, as through water. He said that to lie in bed with my hair was like sleeping on the waves."

She paused.

"That was a sweet time in my life."

Grandma laid the paddle across the canoe. She leaned toward me, over the bar between us.

"You have my hair, not your mother's. She was a pretty, fair child. But you have the hair of my mother and grandmother before me. You should let it grow, Meg. Long hair gives a person strength."

She laughed.

"Well," she said, "that's what my grandmother used to say."

Maybe part of your family history has to do with what you've inherited, or a story you've been told about the old days. What do you think you've inherited from your great-grandmother, your grandmother, or your mother? What do you think you've inherited from your father or grandfather? What choices can you make in your life that your foremothers or forefathers didn't make or couldn't make? Would you make any of the same choices? How have you already begun your own journey?

In *Shizuko's Daughter*, by Kyoko Mori, Yuki is growing up without her mother. When Yuki was twelve years old, her mother committed suicide. In this selection from the novel, it's years after her mother's death, and Yuki is talking with Mr. Kimura, who loved Yuki's mother when he and her mother were both young. He's now married to Yuki's aunt, Aya. Yuki tells him

"I believe that if we could foresee the future, none of us would ever fall in love. It comes to nothing one way or the other."

Mr. Kimura leaned back against the tree, his arms folded. He seemed to be thinking for a long time. Finally, he said, "When I was younger and my marriage was going badly, I used to think the same thing too. What's the point? It all turns out badly. I felt that way again when I heard about your mother's death. I was forty then. But in the last few years, as I've gotten to be forty-five and forty-six, I began to think differently. I think now that it's worth it all the same, loving someone. It may not turn out right, but I want to love someone in spite of it. In a way it means more because the odds are against us. If I didn't think that, I would never have married Aya."

Yuki tried to imagine it — herself at forty-five feeling that love was worthwhile. It was difficult. All she could think of was herself running around the track, a fast lap, a slow lap, endlessly, while the others fell in love.

Yuki's feelings about love change when her father gives her a sketchbook of her mother's he has saved. It's filled with pictures in watercolor and pencil of Yuki and her father. As she looks through them, Yuki thinks again about love, her parents, and her future.

In the middle part of the sketchbook, Yuki saw sketch after sketch of herself done in pencil. The strokes were swift but careful. In the later pictures, she recognized some of the clothes, toys, places. . . .

On the second-to-last page, Yuki found a detailed watercolor portrait of herself holding some daisies to her nose and smiling a big, frank smile. . . . This is how my mother saw me, she thought, such a happy child. . . . We were happy, Yuki thought; anybody could tell.

She turned to the last page. It was a pencil sketch of her father sleeping on the chaise lounge in the cottage. Her mother's pencil strokes were at once bold and careful. She must have been eager to sketch him before he woke up. Several hydrangea blossoms had been pressed right onto the page. . . .

(H)e looked slightly sullen but almost comical, endearing even. . . . This is how she wanted to see him, Yuki thought. . . . She even pressed these flowers to the last page of her sketchbook. . . . She must have loved him still.

Yuki closed the sketchbook and put it on the bed. She wondered when her mother had stopped loving her father, what she would say if Yuki could ask her now, "Did you regret loving him?" Mr. Kimura had said . . . . that he wanted to love someone even if it ended in sadness. . . . But love brings sadness, Yuki thought, even when the other person doesn't hurt you on purpose. . . .

Yuki closed the sketchbook and held it on her lap. My mother, she thought, wanted to be . . . . at the center of my mind, almost swallowed up by the light around it but always there. She would want me to look beyond her unhappiness.

How do you think Yuki can do what she says her mother wants her to do, "to look beyond her [mother's] unhappiness"? What suggestions would you make to Yuki about her future? Have you ever tried to be different from your mother? Have you ever tried to be the same as your mother? From either or both, what have you learned about being yourself?

What makes you happy? Can you list your happiest times? What makes you sad? Can you list your saddest times? What role has love — being loved or loving other people — played in either or both?

The last story is about a girl living in Europe. In *Over the Water,* by Maude Casey, fourteen-year-old Mary Maeve calls her mother Mammy. Mary was born in London and her mother, who is Irish Catholic, is very strict with her.

The family goes to Ireland to visit Mammy's farm and family. Life in the Irish countryside is confusing for Mary, who takes to her bed for days on end. Her aunt brings her a book of Irish folklore, about a nearby place called Tir na N'Og, and the first Maeve, who was a queen. Mary struggles to understand why her mother named her Maeve after such a powerful woman at the same time that her mother doesn't seem to want her to be powerful.

When Mammy comes into the bedroom, I feel myself become tight all over. She fires desperate questions at me, so that my magic land recedes and her anxiety replaces it, clawing at me. When she pulls back the curtain and says, "It's a grand day!" I know that it's an accusation, and what she really means is, "Why aren't you out in the sunshine?"

She confuses me so much, with her code of words that mean different things from what they actually say. My head loses its lightness and clarity when I'm with her, so that I find myself hurtling words at her like cannonballs. And before I know where I am, I am struggling in tangled threads and I don't even know myself any longer what it is I'm trying to say . . . .

One morning Mary Maeve decides to leave her room. It's early, and she sees a colt. As she gets closer to him, she decides she's going to ride him through the same forests the Maeve of Irish history lived in.

Shivering, I turn the colt back onto the track and continue toward the mountain. I am glad of the sun upon my back. I am glad of the warm moving body of the horse against my legs. What a shame it is that Mammy is afraid of horses. I wonder if she has ever walked this way? . . . .

I am dreamy and spellbound. The elusive magic of Tir na N'Og is all around me, and inside me, too. The whole land is alive with it. The cattle in the field beyond, lifting their heads as we pass, are like fairy cattle, belly-high in wild flowers and grasses. The mountain is changing color again. Two small wispy clouds are hanging gaily over its summit.

My belly is heavy and warm with my period. I clench and unclench my legs against the muscles of the colt. I am making my body work after so long. . . .

I am strong and calm. There is no distance between me and everything surrounding me. . . . There is no ending; everything is continuing. The whole land is alive, and the air above it. . . .

I have seen enough. I know now that it takes longer than an afternoon to reach a mountain. And that the land of your dreams might be the very one you're walking through. Curling my fingers in the tangle of his mane, I turn the colt back on himself and I head for home. . . .

I am luckier than any of the people who have gone before me. I do not have to work all my days in a numbing battle against poverty and sickness, in a struggle to bring up children in a world that denies them even food or warmth. I do not have to be a victim of circumstance. . . .

Yes, that's it! I have a choice. I do not have to be a victim of circumstances, of my parents' anger, or of anybody's expectations for me! I decided to take to my bed, and now I have decided to get up. I did that, and now I can decide to show them all that I am capable of making sensible decisions. The colt has come to no harm.

As we turn from the track and turn into the lane, I look back and say "Thank you." Then I see our house above the trees ahead of me. And as we start to trot down the lane, my heart is singing with its first real song of freedom.

This is a very beautiful description of a ride through the Irish countryside. Have you experienced anything that makes you feel as good as Mary feels? What makes you feel free? Perhaps you can sketch or write about your place of freedom. Freedom makes me think of my green stone, and liking myself.

Mary's feeling of freedom could stay with her all her life. What predictions would you make for her when she's a woman? How do you feel about growing up? Talking to other girls and women about their feelings and experiences about becoming women may inspire you to write or draw about your future.

When you grow up, you'll be your true self as a grown-up. All the years you've lived are a part of who you'll become, just as Sandra Cisneros described what it means to be eleven with the experiences and feelings of the first ten years inside you.

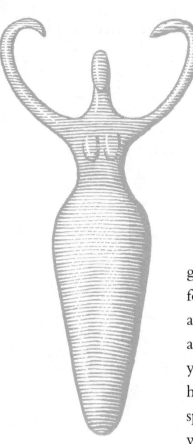

We've reached the time in the second session when girls and women write about their true selves. It's time for you to read what they have to say about who they are. They may make you think about how you feel now and what being a unique person — no matter how old you are — means to you. After reading this section, you have an opportunity to write about who you are, in that special place inside you that no one else knows, and what you have or haven't discovered so far.

To Be Powerful
by Shakoiya, 11

I believe in speaking my mind and telling people what I feel and what I think and not to bite my tongue. What I mean is if someone is doing something to you, you should let them know about it before it gets worse. So always speak your mind and that's when you're powerful. And never let any man or woman take advantage of you.

An Adventurous Self
by Iesha, 12

My true self is taking a nap and doesn't want to be disturbed. But I can tell you how she is. She's adventurous and loves scary stuff.

My Green Stone
by Katie, 11

I think my true self is goofy and happy.

My True Self
by Toni, 13

I haven't found mine yet. She's very quiet, but she's in there. I can feel her.

Disappearing Acts
by Kizzy, 16

The world is just too fussy for
    me,
But I think I'm too bold for it.
There's nothing to understand
And someone to relate to.
But why don't they understand
Who I am inside.
The fact that I work hard at
    everything
And I do all that I can
So they could comprehend.
There is no such thing as foolish
    pride
For if there was then people
    would
Feel so empty
Trying to accomplish goals.
I see that I can't help so
I swallow up and disappear, for
I hate to be wrong or unwanted.
There's no one to hear my silent
    cries

Because no one was ever really
   listening.
I had too much to say anyway
But then again nothing at all.
So while others act like they
   were there
I turn around and disappear.

Who I am, Who I'm Becoming
by Carolyn, 22

I believe that I am strong-willed and am-
bitious, destined to be powerful. Powerful to
me means being myself and being happy with
myself. I describe myself as intelligent, adventurous and versatile. I strive to have a career and a family. I believe in being true to
myself and living with no regrets. I find good
in all.

In 22 years, I believe I have come full circle
with certain aspects of my life, but there are
many circles to be completed. My true self is
capable of being child-like, but grown up and
responsible. When necessary, I'm giving, caring

and sometimes even selfish. Being true means being honest even if it means admitting the negative and accepting what I can't change.

I wish I could be more open and express myself. Anger is easier to express than hurt and sadness. I'm trying to become someone who is more open. Although people say I can be stubborn, that's okay. Stubborn can be positive if it means keeping your own ideas and pursuing your dreams.

Being Reborn
by Rebecca, 46

I am going to be forty-seven years old and I am being reborn. I am scared. I did what I was supposed to do: that was get married, have children, stay home and take care of the house. But something went wrong, something that wasn't supposed to happen. Something I wasn't told could happen.

I was suddenly a widow, left with two children. I thought I was alone on this huge planet. But I am not alone. I have myself.

My True Self: Feelings Deeply
Expressed By Myself
by Keosha, 12

The real me inside is full of joy, love, and happiness. I'm full of love because you have to love yourself before you can love anyone else and I love myself and everybody.

I'm filled with happiness because I'm happy with whatever I do to make myself happy. I'm filled with joy.

My True Self
by Tammie, 33

I, Tammie, am a very special person in my own way. I love everybody regardless of color or who they are. I am a very loving and caring person who wants everything under the sun for my kids. My two girls are everything to me. I am down in a rut right now because I really love my husband, but he has a problem that I can't deal with. I have stood behind him for four years.

So now Tammie is ready to go on with her new life and enjoy her children and relax. Stop being that other person and stand up for herself.

My True Self
by Sibley, 26
My true self is a dappled green
light through a leafy canopy
limitless as water,
bright as stars.
But I keep forgetting that
and believe I'm tax returns
and back orders
and constant complaints,
that I'm dimples and
dented car fenders
and the annoying, funny
theme songs to TV sitcoms.
Sometimes I think
what I need to do,
rather than what I want to do.
I forget,

in the face of fear,
that I am the face of love.
Just remembering
makes me cry
softly in forgiveness.

What Makes me Feel Powerful
by Cherlnell, 9

When I get an A+ or an A on a test.
When I get told I am smart.
When people tell me I will become some-
thing big.
When people tell me I am strong-willed.
That's what makes me feel powerful.
Strong-willed is independent and brave.
And I'll stay like that forever.

My True Self
by Lydia, age 9 and 7/8

My true self just woke up from a
loooonnngggg cat nap. Now the reason I call
it a cat nap is because I believe I was always

sorta awake. What do I mean by that? Well, when I get my feelings hurt, my true self tells me not to get mad at the person who hurt my feelings.

But today it really woke up. It turned me into a person who pretty much does what I want unless my Mom tells me not to, then I try to be content with out it. Good night, true self.

My True Self
by Sierra, 10

My true self is someone who cares and someone who helps. And is sweet and very interesting.

I show my inner self when something tragic happens and also when something that isn't tragic happens.

My true self really believes that I'm not embarrassed about my dyslexia because it's my true self.

I'm also very artistic and I like to paint stuff.

My True Self
by Lizzy, 10 3/4

A lot of people think one personality in you is who you really are. But I think, at least, my inner self is many personalities swirled together, to become me!

I think I have a great singer inside me, wanting to push out, let go — but somehow it's having a lot of trouble. . . . The reason, I think, that my inner-singer-self-person is having trouble getting out is that, when it's about to push through, I'm criticized. "You sing too loud!" "Stop singing, I'm trying to talk." "STOP singing, I'm trying to study!" over and over again.

My inner self is my family, my friend that I can trust. . . . My family's history. MY history. MY innerself is ME!

A Special Person
by Melissa, 11

My true self is being generous. I enjoy giving things to other people. I also enjoy being by myself and just having time to think. I enjoy writing stories. Since I am very imaginative, I daydream a lot. I like to sit and pet my rabbit. I also like to read.

I am an artistic person, I love colors. I draw when I'm bored. I like to talk, although I am usually shy. I am sometimes what other people call "weird." I think I am a special person.

THE END

P.S. Hi, how are you? I am fine.

My True Self
by Carrie, 11

My true self is someone I can't really put my finger on, but I know I'm loving, caring, funny, and I'm really social. I can make friends with just about everyone and also always think ahead like what kind of shoes I'm going to wear *to the prom or who I'm going to get married to sometime.*

Wanting to know ahead is good. Other times it's bad. I want to be a lawyer and I'm already starting to learn the things you have to learn. So far, I like it . . . .

My True Self
by Brittany, 11 1/2

I think my true self is a kind, loving, talkative person. I am a wonderful equestrian (horse rider). When I get on a horse, I can just <u>ride</u>! I'm never nervous, I just know inside that I can jump the three-foot jump.

I also have a wonderful memory. I can remember things from a long time ago. My inner self has a tendency to love animals. When I'm around them I feel so . . . great! It's like I become one when I'm around one. That's why when I grow up I want to be a veterinarian.

In addition, I love to draw horses or just anything else. Drawing always makes me feel so relaxed....

My very last thing is that I love to shop. I'm always myself when I shop. I know where to go, and how to get there. I just love to shop — and talk.

My True Self
by Diana, 41

My true self's name is Dicey, which is my childhood name and the one all my friends use. As I got older, and entered the "professional" and adult world, I was encouraged to put away my childish things — this included the persona of Dicey.

But she still exists and when I need to be myself, I can always go where she is, and without too much effort, bring my true self out and really be the child-girl-woman I want to be.

My True Self
by Susan, 46

My true self hurts when anyone else hurts. What is difficult for me is to remember that people who lash out, are mean, cruel or angry, are really hurting.

I'll cry at the drop of a hat when I hear music or see someone in pain. But I love to laugh, and nothing is more special than laughing so hard with your head thrown back and tears down your cheeks.

I cherish quiet, trees, peace, children, animals and special parties when people are their true selves.

Planet Escapism
by Crystal, 16

My true self's name is Crystal. My true self does not want to grow up. Being an adult does not appeal to me. It's too complicated. Too much stuff to remember. Too much pressure. Yeah, that's it.

My true self likes simple things. Nothing complicated. Simple like childhood where everything is on your terms.

My true self hates change. My true self loves happiness, but isn't happy all of the time. My true self (contrary to popular beliefs) is very intelligent. My true self loves to be tickled. My true self loves little kids, but don't tell anyone. They may think the outside me is soft.

My true self likes to escape. To touch the sky on swings. . . .

Come.
Follow.
Line up.
You are all sheep.
"Not I!" said Crystal (the true self).

Who I Am
by Adeola, 16

I am a very sensitive person at times. Sometimes what people say to me can really mean a lot. I often sit by myself and think, really think about my life. When I think about me, I cry sometimes because it really shows that I really care about myself and actually worry about my future.

When I'm not by myself, I'm usually with my friends or my boyfriend. I like to talk about anything and like going anywhere.... If something really hits me or I am really deeply interested, that's when I speak out.

I find myself to be a caring person and I am always there to listen. I don't really confide in anybody about anything. I usually keep things to myself. I haven't really found anyone I can trust enough with my feelings. I love myself though, and I love being the true me.

Finding Out Who I Am
by Elizabeth, 12

Today, I am strong. I almost feel like I could take on the world. I strive on strength. But also on caring and love. It just occurred to me that I am actually a strong woman. Yes, I do feel I am a woman now though I haven't gotten my period yet.

I do not feel you need your period to become a woman. That is usually the most important part. But to me it is simply physical. I am not saying that your period is not important in your life. It's just that it is not as important as most other things.

I feel that I have become a woman mentally. That I have found maturity without losing the part of me that I love. My imagination, my dreams, myself. I have made it all the way into eighth-grade without becoming merely an object for the public. For that, I am special. I have seen many girls fall into that horrible fate. I know it will never happen to me. I am my very own special self. With my young girl still lovingly inside when I grow up and physi-

cally mature. I am different and strong, but special.

What I Feel My True Self Is?
by Anisah, 16

I don't really know who my true self is at this point in my life. I'm young and in high school. Most of my waking hours are spent studying to get good grades and get a good scholarship so I can be somebody important (meaning professionally). I feel my true self is a person who is quiet and talkative, understanding and selfish, I'm tons of things, good and bad.

I feel that I listen to people's problems too much so that I don't really have time to think about me and only me. When I'm by myself I feel like I should be doing something to help others. Sometimes I feel I am just going to burn out from listening to people. Not that I don't love the people, but what about me and my pain and my loneliness.

And before this day I never really thought about my true self. And now I feel I want to know and that I will take time to find out about who I am.

The Real Me
by Cara, 16

Crazy
Weird
Happy
Sad
Angry
Lonely
Friendly
Can party all night long
Listens to all types of music
Spiritual
All of these things make up the
Real Me.

My True Self
by Nenee, 24

I don't believe I have just one true self. There are many, but I only know or am aware of but a few. Those few I can count on one hand.

For years I've known the self that motivates me to live life to the fullest, to fulfill my dreams. The self that everybody else needs, as well as myself. The self that is unstoppable and demanding.

Lately, the past month or so, I've encountered a self that I'm not too sure I like, but to some extent do like and appreciate because it is me. This self isn't so much a scared me, but the one that isn't as strong or powerful. In fact, it's weak and lonely. The side that isn't independent. The side that will latch on, latch onto someone I love. I'm not used to this self. And so, the self I've always been and lived by is in constant battle with its opposite.

What has occurred has taught me something. That my journey for self will not always be a pleasant one. But in the end, it will only *(or so I hope) make me stronger . . . allow me to be only one — Nenee.*

Who Am I?
by Cindy, 17

I really am not too sure. Sometimes I feel lost, and go crazy. Sometimes I just don't know if I am someone at all. My true self is very hidden. I may try to bring it out, but it is very hard for me. Sometimes thinking about myself makes me very sad, because I feel as if my life is falling apart. Everything seems so twisted and upside down for me.

I think I should start thinking about myself and stop thinking about other people, because they are not really thinking of me. Only I can think of myself, and only I know exactly who I am, nobody else.

The things that I think make me a young woman are my heart, mind, and body. These things control me, and build up my self-esteem, and help me to know who I am. Last, but not least, I am sexy, sweet, honest, truthful, loving, caring and sharing.

All these things are what make me who I am and a young, black, intelligent woman.

But I Wouldn't
by Christina, 12

When I wake up,
Well, I know I'm gonna be,
I'm gonna be the girl
Who wakes up free from drugs.
When I go out,
Yeah, I know I'm gonna be,
I'm gonna be the girl
Who walks away from drugs.
If I don't take them,
Yeah, I know I'm gonna be,
I'm gonna be the girl
Who's stronger than the rest.

But I wouldn't smoke any laced-up joint,
And I wouldn't do any other drug,
Just to be the kid who fits in with all the
   rest of Those doped up kids.

Who My True Self Is
by Shaniqua, 16

My true self has not been totally developed yet. There is much I must strive to learn about who I really am. Day by day, when I think, I discover more of who I really am. Sometimes what I do one day contradicts what I might do another day. My self is like the seasons, always changing, never staying long enough to be caught.

Sometimes I think real hard to try to define who I am, what I stand for or what I believe. When I do this what happens is the things I encounter daily cloud the true image of who I am, what I am becoming and what I'm trying to be.

I could give you a long definition of me. I could say "Shaniqua is like this and likes this," but am I really describing all the true attributes of me. Good with the bad? In reality, I'm still digging because there's something inside me, still trying to define itself.

What I am is a caterpillar in a cocoon or a baby in a womb or a coal under pressure. The end result will be true and beautiful, but now I'm in the metamorphic process. My life will center around reaching that point or goal within me. When I reach it, I'll stand tall and proud, expressing and delighting in my true self.

My True Self
by Courtney, 16

I really don't know, but I have some idea. I think that I'm a really nurturing person to others, but I don't express this on myself. I think I have a purpose on this earth, but I haven't quite figured it out yet. Maybe I'm not supposed to know yet, but it would be nice if I get some kind of sign.

It seems like I'm a nothing, meaning-less, and empty. Like I'm supposed to help, or please others, but neglect my-self. I also feel out of place, and lonely at times. Like no one understands me. I know I'm supposed to feel fortunate be-cause I'm loved and have shelter, but there are other things that I need and want without being called selfish.

My True Self
by Kristina, 9

My true self is lonely, happy, sad, nice, mean, pretty, ugly, scared, surprised, and funny. When I say I'm ugly, it means I'm bad, pretty means I'm good.

And I am all of the words I said all the time at the same time. You may not know it, but deep down inside me I am.

When the girls and women have finished writing about their true selves, there's a lot of excitement in the room. Sometimes we get up and move around, clear the room of pencils, pens, and paper, and then we form a circle with some of us sitting and some of us stretched out on the floor. Different conversations erupt around the circle.

What feelings do you have when you hear other girls' words about their true selves? Have you found ways to be yourself that you can share? When you think of something, however large or small, put it down in your journal.

Some girls are eager to make promises to themselves. In Chicago, for instance, we stood in a circle and each person made a promise. One girl said, "I'll always remember there are girls and women who'll be there for me." Another said, "I'll hold onto my dream no matter what happens."

What makes you feel safe? What scares you? Do you know anyone who was able to continue her life and make it better after a tragic thing happened?

Maybe you have strong feelings about someone or something that you'd like to write or draw about. You may want to write a letter even if you decide not to mail it. Maybe just writing your feelings down will help — and you can share it when you're ready.

It's almost time to finish this last session of "Girls Speak Out."

If we were in the same room, I think we'd notice that

everyone is looking a little sad at the thought of leaving. I know when I look around the room — or right now, when I'm imagining you reading these words — I think about the strength and independence of all the girls I've met. It inspires me to be my best self and to have faith in the future. I'm so glad we've spent this time together.

The last book we read is our second picture book. It's called *Zora Hurston and the Chinaberry Tree.* The author is William Miller and the pictures are watercolors painted by a husband and wife team, Ying-Hwa Hu and Cornelius Van Wright. The pictures are mostly in greens and browns, and the young Zora looks like a warm and lively young girl.

Zora Hurston was a writer who wrote about her own people, the people she was proudest of, black Americans. She collected folklore about African-American life, and wrote novels, short stories, and books of anthropology. Alice Walker, author of *Finding the Green Stone,* says she "needed" Zora's writings because they told stories she hadn't found in literature before. They are universal, and all of us can learn from them.

Zora had a hard life as a writer. One of the reasons was that she was using an unusual voice in her writing, that of "ordinary" Southern black people instead of the speech in books. Zora used folkspeech instead of standard English.

People couldn't accept something else that is clear in Zora's work: that blacks are a proud and daring people who have survived their struggles in a patriarchy.

Zora died penniless in a welfare home in Florida. When Alice read that Zora's grave didn't have a marker on it, she went to Florida to do what felt like a "duty" to another black woman writer: in a cemetery overgrown with weeds, Alice found what she thought was Zora's grave. She had a headstone put on it that says:

ZORA NEALE HURSTON
"A GENIUS OF THE SOUTH"
NOVELIST FOLKLORIST
ANTHROPOLOGIST
1901   1960

Telling you this story about Alice and Zora brings together two voices that inspire us to be our true selves. Zora makes me believe, as she wrote in *Their Eyes Are Watching God,* that I can wrap the horizon around me, and as Zora says, the horizon is the biggest thing on this earth.

Zora spent her childhood in a small town called Eatonville, in Florida, where her father was mayor.

Eatonville was the first all-black, incorporated town in America, and she learned a pride in her own people that lasted all her life. From her mother, she also learned something very important — as you'll see. Each of her parents had something different to teach her.

In *Zora Hurston and the Chinaberry Tree,* Zora is a young girl looking for *her* voice:

Zora Hurston loved the chinaberry tree.

Her mother taught her to climb it, one
branch at a time.
From the tree, she could see as far
as the lake, as far as the horizon . . . .

Zora dreamed of seeing the cities beyond
the horizon, of living there one day.

But only boys fished in the lake,
only men traveled to the cities.
Zora watched with envy as the wagons
rattled down the dusty roads.

Her father told her to wear a dress, ...
He warned her about girls who didn't obey
their fathers, girls who didn't grow up to be
young ladies.

But Zora only listened to her mother.

She taught Zora that everything had a voice:
the trees and rushing wind, the stars
in the midnight sky.

She taught Zora that the world belonged
to her, even the lake and far-off horizon.

So Zora went everywhere. . . .

She followed boys to the edge of campfires,
listened while their fathers sang about John Henry . . .

Zora learned about Africa, the place where
she and her people came from.

In Africa they had been kings and queens,
builders of cities that stood for thousands of years. . . .

One morning Zora's mother didn't feel well.

She told Zora not to worry . . .
She told Zora to go
outside and play, to climb her favorite tree.

But Zora couldn't play. She saw how tired
her mother was . . .

Day after day, Zora sat beside her mother's bed
telling her the stories she had heard
beside the campfires.

Her mother smiled and asked Zora to always
remember what she had learned.

Stories, she said, kept their people alive.
As long as they were told, Africa would live
in their hearts.
Zora promised to remember.

Zora's mother slowly got worse.
Men and women came to sit up with her
through the long, hot nights. . . .

Zora was sitting in the parlor when her
father told her she would not see her
mother again.

Zora felt as if she had died. She watched while the old
people stopped the clocks, put sheets on the mirror.

She watched while the women cried and the men
stared at their Sunday shoes.
But then she could sit still no more.

Where do you think Zora is going? Where would you go? What would you do?

Zora ran from the house, ran all the way
to the chinaberry tree.

Did you guess Zora was going to the chinaberry tree? Is there a special place you and a family member or someone else you love share? Any place you look forward to escaping to? Maybe when you've finished reading about Zora, you could write about or sketch your special place.

She climbed the first branch and the next,
climbed almost to the top.

A sparrow sang to her in a voice like her
mother's. The sparrow told her
not to give up, to climb even higher.

From the top of the tree Zora saw again
the world her mother had given her:
the lake filled with fish, the cities where she would
tell people all she had learned . . .

Zora promised her mother that she would
never stop climbing,

would always reach for the newborn sky,
always jump at the morning sun!

What promise would you make to yourself? Why do you think we make promises to ourselves? Do you think it was important for Zora to climb, even after her mother's death? How would you describe Zora's true self?

Our closing discussion in "Girls Speak Out" is about the power of each person to make a difference. Each voice we've heard, whether it's our own voice, another girl's or woman's voice, live or from literature, is unique.

Each voice matters.

When we join our voices, we hear all the possibilities around us. We want to do something about keeping our voices clear and loud, and making them heard.

Are you trying to do something to change your school or your neighborhood or any part of your world for the better? Then you've already started your adventure from the inside out.

Will you organize "Girls Speak Out" sessions? How will you use the information in this book?

Will you continue to write and draw? How do you

feel about showing your work to other people, or maybe one day publishing it?

What has changed in you after reading this book?

Doing "Girls Speak Out" sessions and writing this book encouraged me to ask and answer some questions about my own girlhood. I've spent the last two years exploring the good and bad things I experienced while growing up. It might be helpful for you to know that I discovered, when I looked deep inside myself, there was no secret "waiting to get me." I used to think I had something inside me I didn't want to know about or that wasn't as good as other people. Some of the girls who wrote about their true selves had a similar feeling.

Now I've found my true self, and I'm glad I can be who I always wanted to be.

When we created "Girls Speak Out," Gloria and I knew we had lost some of our true selves as we were growing up. We tried to make things better for other people, especially girls and women, but sometimes we got out of balance by paying more attention to other people than to ourselves. Each of us found our true selves again when we were in our early fifties. So you see, it's never too late.

But when we were your age, there wasn't a women's movement to let us know that the patriarchy was the problem, not us.

Now, you don't have to grow up feeling there's something wrong with you. Or that you're the only one who feels the way you do.

We know that girls can resist losing their true selves as they grow up.

You can be your true self all your life.

Closings and Beginnings

By the end of the last session, we have a book of our writings and our memories. When you close this book, you'll have it and your memories, too.

We can't see our true selves, just as we can't see each other right now. Like words, our true selves touch and connect us even when we're not in the same room.

We'll be together each time we remember how strong and independent each girl and woman is. When we see a green stone in our imagination or in our hand, we are looking at a symbol of each of us, a unique combination of our ancestors, ourselves, and our future.

If we were together in the same room, we'd play the Tunnels game, giving each other permission to go.

We'd go out the door laughing and hugging each other. I'd watch the last girl leave as I pack my books and papers.

But . . . .

You and I met in these pages. We don't have to say good-bye the way we would in person.

Let's try this:

As you end this book, think about your green stone. Think about all the green stones shining inside girls and women.

Now . . . please read the words below.

I hope they make you smile, too.

Our green stones remind us we can do things no one else can,

Because we're each unique and special,

But we're all connected to each other

And to the biggest green stone of all:

The Earth.

About the
Ancient Artifacts

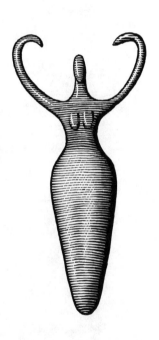

1. This Nile River goddess is an inside-out image to a lot of girls because her arms resemble the Fallopian tubes. She's an ancient African symbol of the overflowing female body and spirit.

2. The Cretan Snake Goddess was found in a palace on Crete, an island that is the same distance between Europe and Africa. She's about 3900 years old and it's believed that she understood the snake, a powerful image of rebirth who sheds its skin.

3. The Willendorf Goddess is approximately 30,000 years old and she was found in Europe. She's one of the oldest sculptures of a human, and she is designed to be hand-held or placed in the ground to stand.

4. When girls hold this ancient Greek figure they often have the same idea: she looks like a "cramps doll" because of the position of her hands and knees. She's about 4800 years old and was found in tombs.

5. Approximately 6000 years old, this image of a dreaming woman was found on an island in the Mediterranean. Some believe that a Neolithic goddess culture existed in the caves where she was found, and that their wisdom was found in dreams.

6. Kuan Yin is an ancient Chinese goddess who reminds us that peace comes from the inside out. She is a thinker known for her compassion and forgiveness.

7. This gentle figure who seems wrapped up in herself stands upright and her arms extend into snake-like coils that wrap around her body. This European statue has a face whose lack of features reminds us that we are all one female.

8. This woman is a European crone goddess. A crone is an old, wise woman. Old age is a time of power. She, too, understands the snake.

9. This is an Eskimo image that faces in two directions. Some believe that the bowl-like surface was like a candle: a place where things are burned to celebrate an important event.

10. This African image is made from wood and is a popular female figure. She was believed to be carried both by women who wanted to have children, as well as by women who didn't want to bear children, but who would carry — and dance with — this figure instead.

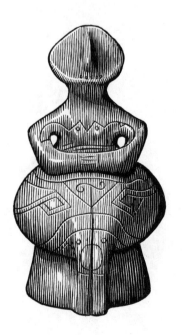

11. This figure appears to be seated on a throne, but it's really her body that resembles a throne. She's thought to symbolize Mother Earth. This artifact is approximately 4500 years old. She is European.

12. This tiny figure is European and is called a votive figure, one of thousands found like her. She, too, fits easily in a hand, but she also stands upright and statues like her were found standing all around ancient rooms.

13. This is a piece of a wall carving which is thought to be European. The goddess is carved with animals and is holding symbols of the harvest. Ancient images of females were often associated with life, including the earth's gift of other forms of life.

Further Reading

Allen, Paula Gunn, ed. *Spider Woman's Granddaughters: Traditional Tales and Contemporary Writing by Native American Women.* (Beacon, 1989).

Alvarez, Julia. *How the Garcia Girls Lost Their Accents.* (Algonquin, 1991).

Angelou, Maya. *I Know Why the Caged Bird Sings.* (Bantam, 1969).

Atkinson, Linda. *In Kindling Flame: The Story of Hannah Senesh.* (Lothrop, 1985).

Atwood, Margaret. *Cat's Eye.* (Doubleday, 1989); *Handmaid's Tale.* (Fawcett, 1986).

Avi. *The True Confessions of Charlotte Doyle.* (Orchard, 1990).

Bauer, Marion Dane. *Am I Blue.* (Harper, 1994).

Boyd, Candy Dawson. *Breadsticks and Blessing Places.* (Macmillan, 1985).

Brainard, Cecilia M. *When The Rainbow Goddess Wept.* (Dutton, 1994).

Busby, Margaret. *Daughters of Africa.* (Ballantine, 1992).

Byars, Betsy. *The Moon and I.* (Messner, 1991).

Chang, Ida. *A Separate Battle: Women and the Civil War.* (Lodestar, 1991).

Childress, Alice. *Rainbow Jordan.* (Putnam, 1981).

Choi, Sook Nyul. *Year of Impossible Goodbyes.* (Houghton Mifflin, 1991).

Cisneros, Sandra. *The House on Mango Street.* (Random House, 1989).

Cleary, Beverly. *A Girl from Yamhill: A Memoir.* (Morrow, 1988).

Cohen, Barbara. *People Like Us.* (Bantam, 1987).

Cole, Brock. *Celine.* (Farrar, Straus & Giroux, 1989).

Conrad, Pam. *Prairie Songs.* (HarperCollins, 1985).

Conway, Jill Kerr. *Written by Herself.* (Vintage, 1992); *Road from Coorain.* (Vintage, 1990).

Crew, Linda. *Children of the River.* (Delacorte, 1989).

Cushman, Karen. *Catherine Called Birdy.* (Clarion, 1994).

Dana, Barbara. *Young Joan.* (HarperCollins, 1991).

Deaver, Julie. *Say Goodnight, Gracie.* (HarperCollins, 1988).

Dickinson, Peter. *Eva.* (Delacorte, 1989).

Doherty, Berlie. *Granny Was a Buffer Girl.* (Orchard, 1986).

Dorris, Michael. *Morning Girl.* (Hyperion, 1992).

Farman, Farmaian. *Daughter of Persia: A Woman's Journey from Her Father's Harem Through the Islamic Revolution.* (Crown, 1992).

Freedman, Russell. *Eleanor Roosevelt: A Life of Discovery.* (Clarion, 1993).

Fritz, Jean. *Homesick: My Own Story.* (Putnam, 1982).

Furlong, Monica. *Wise Child.* (Knopf, 1987); *Juniper.* (Knopf, 1991).

Garden, Nancy. *Annie on My Mind.* (Farrar, Straus & Giroux, 1982).

Garrique, Sheila. *The Eternal Spring of Mr. Ito.* (Bradbury, 1985).

George, Jean Craighead. *Julie.* (HarperCollins, 1994).

Grant, Cynthia. *Uncle Vampire.* (Atheneum, 1993).

Green, Rayna. *Women in American Indian Society.* (Chelsea House, 1992).

Hamilton, Virginia. *Cousins.* (Putnam, 1990); *Sweet Whispers, Brother Rush.* (Putnam, 1982).

Hesse, Karen. *Letters from Rifka.* (Holt, 1992).

Ho, Minfong. *Rice Without Rain.* (Lothrop, 1990).

Houston, Jeanne Wakatsuki and James. *Farewell to Manzanar.* (Bantam, 1973).

Hurston, Zora Neale. *Their Eyes Were Watching God.* (HarperCollins, 1990).

Jenkins, Lyll Becerra de. *The Honorable Prison.* (Dutton, 1988).

Johnston, Morna. *Louisa May: The World & Works of Louisa May Alcott.* (Macmillan, 1991).

Jukes, Mavis. *Getting Even.* (Knopf, 1988); *Wild Iris Bloom.* (Knopf, 1992).

Kerr, M.E. *Me Me Me Me Me: Not a Novel.* (Harper, 1983).

Kincaid, Jamaica. *Annie John.* (Farrar, Straus & Giroux, 1983).

Kingston, Maxine Hong. *The Woman Warrior.* (Random House, 1976).

Klein, Norma. *Just Friends.* (Knopf, 1990).

Konigsburg, E.L. *T-Backs, T-Shirts, Coat and Suit.* (Atheneum, 1993).

Lasky, Kathryn. *Beyond the Divide.* (Macmillan, 1983).

Lee, Marie. *Finding My Voice.* (Houghton, 1992).

Levitin, Sonia. *The Return.* (Atheneum, 1987).

Lowry, Lois. *Number the Stars.* (Houghton, 1989).

Lyons, Mary. *Letters From a Slave Girl.* (Scribner, 1992); *Sorrow's Kitchen.* (Macmillan, 1990).

Machlachlan, Patricia. *Facts & Fictions of Minna Pratt.* (Harper, 1988).

Mahy, Margaret. *The Catalogue of the Universe.* (Scholastic, 1986).

Makeba, Miriam. *Makeba: My Story.* (NAL/Plume, 1988).

Mazer, Norma Fox. *After the Rain.* (Morrow, 1987); *Out of Control.* (1993).

McCunn, Ruthanne Lum. *Thousand Pieces of Gold.* (Design Enterprises, 1981).

McKinley, Robin. *Beauty: Retelling of Beauty & the Beast.* (HarperCollins, 1978).

Morrison, Toni. *Beloved.* (Knopf, 1987).

Namjoshi, Suniti. *Feminist Fables.* (Sheba Feminist Publisher, 1981).

Naylor, Gloria. *The Women of Brewster Place.* (Penguin, 1982).

Naylor, Phyllis Reynolds. *Alice in Rapture, Sort of.* (Atheneum, 1990).

Ng, Fae Myenne. *Bone.* (Hyperion, 1993).

O'Dell, Scott. *Sing Down the Moon.* (Houghton, 1970).

Okimoto, Jean. *Molly By Any Other Name.* (Scholastic, 1990).

O'Neal, Zibby. *In Summer Light.* (Viking, 1985).

Ortiz-Cofer, Judith. *Silent Dancing.* (Arte Publico, 1980).

Parks, Rosa and Haskin, James. *Rosa Parks: My Story.* (Dial, 1992).

Paterson, Katherine. *Lyddie.* (Lodestar, 1991); *Jacob Have I Loved.* (Harper, 1980).

Piekarski, Vicki. ed. *Westward the Women.* (Doubleday, 1984).

Porte, Barbara. *I Only Made Up the Roses.* (Greenwillow, 1987).

Pullman, Philip. *Ruby in the Smoke.* (Knopf, 1987).

Rappaport, Doreen. *Living Dangerously.* (HarperCollins, 1991).

Rinaldi, Ann. *The Story of Tempe Wick.* (Harcourt, 1991).

Russell, Diana. *Lives of Courage: Women for a New South Africa.* (Basic, 1989).

Rylant, Cynthia. *Missing May.* (Orchard, 1992).

Sachs, Marilyn. *The Fat Girl.* (Dutton, 1983).

St. George, Judith. *Dear Dr. Bell. Your Friend, Helen Keller.* (Putnam, 1992).

San Souci, Robert. *Cut From the Same Cloth: American Women of Myth, Legend, and Tall Tales.* (Philomel, 1993.)

Shaaban, Bouthania. *Both Right and Left Handed: Arab Women Talk About Their Lives.* (Indiana University Press, 1991).

Sills, Leslie. *Inspirations.* (Whitman, 1989).

Snyder, Zilpha Keatley. *Libby on Wednesday.* (Doubleday, 1990).

Staples, Suzanne Fisher. *Shabanue.* (Knopf, 1989); *Haveli.* (Knopf, 1993).

Stetogff, Rebecca. *Women of the World.* (Oxford Press, 1992).

Tan, Amy. *The Joy Luck Club* (Putnam, 1989); *Kitchen God's Wife.* (Random House, 1991).

Taylor, Mildred. *Roll of Thunder, Hear My Cry.* (Dial, 1976).

Tsukiyama, Gail. *Women of the Silk.* (St. Martin's Press, 1991).

Turner, Robyn. *Georgia O'Keeffe.* (Little Brown, 1991).

Uchida, Yoshiko. *Invisible Thread* (Messner, 1991); *Picture Bride.* (Fireside, 1987).

Van der Rol, R. & Verhoeven, R. *Anne Frank, Beyond the Diary.* (Viking, 1993).

Voge. Ilse-Margret. *Bad Times, Good Friends.* (Harcourt, 1992).

Voigt, Cynthia. *Homecoming.* (Atheneum, 1981).

Walker, Alice. *In Search of Our Mother's Gardens.* (Harcourt, 1983); *The Color Purple.* (Harcourt, 1982).

Walsh, Jill Patton. *Grace.* (Farrar, 1991).

Walters, Mildred Pitts. *Trouble Child.* (Lothrop, 1985).

Wong, Jade Snow. *Fifth Chinese Daughter.* (Harper, 1950).

Wood, Nancy. *Spirit Walker.* (Doubleday, 1993).

Watkins, Yok Kwashima. *So Far From the Bamboo Grove.* (Lothrop, 1986).

Wrightson, Patricia. *Balyet.* (Macmillan, 1989).

Zheng, Zhensun. *Yani, A Young Painter.* (Scholastic, 1991).

Further Acknowledgments

The author gratefully acknowledges the "Girls Speak Out" program participants whose words appear throughout this book.

Excerpt on pp. 12–16 from *Woman Hollering Creek and Other Stories*, by Sandra Cisneros. Copyright © 1991 by the author. Reprinted by permission of Susan Bergholz Literary Agency.

Excerpt on pp. 30–32 from *Brown Girl, Brownstones*, by Paule Marshall. Copyright © 1981 by the author. Reprinted by permission of the Feminist Press.

Excerpt on pp. 63–66 from *Sojourner Truth: Ain't I a Woman?*, by Patricia C. McKissack and Fredrick L. McKissack. Copyright © 1992 by the authors. Reprinted by permission of Scholastic Press.

Excerpts on pp. 74–78 and pp. 80–82 from *Make Lemonade*, by Virginia Euwer Wolff. Copyright © 1993 by the author. Reprinted by permission of Henry Holt and Company, Inc.

Excerpt on pp. 96–101 from *Finding the Green Stone*, by Alice Walker and Catherine Deeter. Copyright © 1991 by